QUICK AND EASY
SALMON RECIPES

QUICK AND EASY
SALMON RECIPES

Delicious ideas for every occasion, shown
step by step with over 300 photographs

JANE BAMFORTH

southwater

This edition is published by Southwater, an imprint of Anness Publishing Ltd,
Blaby Road, Wigston, Leicestershire LE18 4SE; info@anness.com

www.southwaterbooks.com; www.annesspublishing.com

If you like the images in this book and would like to investigate using them for publishing, promotions or advertising,
please visit our website www.practicalpictures.com for more information.

PUBLISHER: Joanna Lorenz
PROJECT EDITORS: Sarah Ainley and Dan Hurst
COPY EDITOR: Jenni Fleetwood
DESIGNER: Adelle Morris
PRODUCTION CONTROLLER: Wendy Lawson
PHOTOGRAPHY: Tim Auty, Martin Brigdale, Nicki Dowey, James Duncan, Michelle Garrett,
Dave Jordan, David King, Thomas Odulate, William Lingwood and Sam Stowell
ADDITIONAL PHOTOGRAPHY (pp8, 9, 10, 11): The Anthony Blake Photo Library

© Anness Publishing Ltd 2013

A CIP catalogue record for this book is available from the British Library.

NOTES
Bracketed terms are intended for American readers.
For all recipes, quantities are given in both metric and imperial measures and,
where appropriate, in standard cups and spoons.
Follow one set of measures, but not a mixture, because they are not interchangeable.
Standard spoon and cup measures are level. 1 tsp = 5ml, 1 tbsp = 15ml, 1 cup = 250ml/8fl oz.
Australian standard tablespoons are 20ml. Australian readers should use 3 tsp in place of
1 tbsp for measuring small quantities.
American pints are 16fl oz/2 cups. American readers should use 20fl oz/2.5 cups
in place of 1 pint when measuring liquids.
Electric oven temperatures in this book are for conventional ovens.
When using a fan oven, the temperature will probably need to be reduced by about 10–20°C/20–40°F.
Since ovens vary, you should check with your manufacturer's instruction book for guidance.
Medium (US large) eggs are used unless otherwise stated.

Main front cover image shows Salmon Baked with Potatoes and Thyme – for recipe, see page 79.

PUBLISHER'S NOTE
Although the advice and information in this book are believed to be accurate and true at the time of going to
press, neither the authors nor the publisher can accept any legal responsibility or liability for any errors or
omissions that may have been made nor for any inaccuracies nor for any loss, harm or injury
that comes about from following instructions or advice in this book.

CONTENTS

INTRODUCTION

Lovely to look at, delicious and nutritious, salmon makes it a pure pleasure to eat more fish.

Fresh salmon can be served in dozens of different ways – poached, baked, steamed, fried,

grilled (broiled) or cooked on the barbecue. It also stars in soufflés and mousses, pastries and

pasta dishes, sandwiches and salads and makes superb sushi or sashimi. The tasty, varied

recipes in this book, coupled with all the advice on preparing and cooking, will reveal the

enormous versatility of this truly wonderful fish.

TYPES OF SALMON

There are several species of this superb fish, identified initially by the names of the northern oceans in which they spend most of their adult lives. Atlantic salmon are generally judged to have the finest flavour, but the various species of Pacific salmon have their admirers too.

ATLANTIC SALMON (*Salmo salar*)

There is only one species of Atlantic salmon. Its Latin name – *salar* – means leaper, and is a tribute to the creature's athleticism as it travels upstream to the spawning grounds. Atlantic salmon are sleek and muscular, with powerful bodies that contrast with their small heads. On their heads and silvery-blue backs are tiny black crosses. Their sides are silver and the bellies are white. It is quite difficult to tell the sex of immature cock and hen salmon, but during the spawning run, cock salmon develop distinctive hooks or kypes on their lower jaws, making it much easier to tell them apart.

The best salmon are those caught at the start of their spawning run, when they are fat and in prime condition. After leaving the sea, they will not feed again until they return from the spawning grounds, so by the time they get back to sea (if they get back; many salmon die after spawning) they are lean and scrawny.

The average Atlantic salmon weighs about 4.5kg/10lb when mature. The flesh of the wild fish is deep pink in colour, and is firm, succulent and full of flavour.

Salmon roe

The roe of salmon is a beautiful orange-pink colour. It does not have the depth of flavour of sturgeon caviar, but is nonetheless delicious with a squeeze of fresh lemon. The eggs are larger than those of sturgeon and have a delicate, mild flavour and excellent texture. Use them to garnish salmon dishes, or try them with blinis and sour cream. The roe is generally sold in jars, sometimes as *keta*, which is the Russian name for chum salmon.

PACIFIC SALMON (*Oncorhynchus*)

There are six species of Pacific salmon. Five are native to North America and the sixth, masu, is found in Japan.

Sockeye salmon (*Oncorhynchus nerka*)

Slender and silvery when at sea, with blue-black shading on their backs, sockeye salmon are very colourful at the spawning stage. Their heads become olive green and their bodies turn bright red. This has earned them the alternative name of red salmon, and they are also known colloquially as bluebacks. The flesh is an intense red, which is not diminished by canning. Rich and flavourful, it has a high fat content. In the canning industry, sockeye salmon has the highest grade. Smaller than some of the other types of Pacific salmon, sockeyes can weigh as much as 7kg/15½lb, but the average fish on sale is around half this size.

Chinook salmon (*Oncorhynchus tschawytscha*)

Also called the king salmon, this is the largest of the Pacific salmon and takes its common name from the native American tribe for whom they were a vital food source. Chunky in appearance, chinook salmon have silvery bodies with dark backs. These sport sizeable black spots, which are also on the tail. When they spawn, cock chinooks become dark red. The colour is particularly noticeable on the tail fin. The tender, soft-textured flesh ranges from off-white to pinkish-red. The average chinook weighs around 7kg/15½lb, but can grow to over 45kg/100lb.

Coho salmon (*Oncorhynchus kisutch*)

Alternative names for this fish are silver salmon or hooknose, the latter being a reference to the tapered kype or hook that develops on the lower jaw of males during the spawning season. At this stage, too, the silvery sides of cock cohos develop a band of red. Both males and females have small, irregular black spots on the back and tail. The flesh of coho salmon is pinkish orange, with firm texture. It is not as fatty as Chinook or sockeye salmon, and is seldom canned. A popular fish for farming, especially in the north-western United States, cohos are marketed at a weight of around 275g/10oz.

Chum salmon (*Oncorhynchus keta*)

At sea, these slim, elongated fish have silver skins with blue-green backs, without the black spots typical of other species. As they near the spawning season, males develop an olive green hue, and red bands appear on their sides. The pale flesh is lower in fat and not as flavourful as some other varieties. Mature chum salmon weigh around 4.5kg/10lb. Also known as keta, they are widely found in Asian waters.

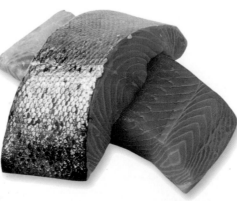

Above: Atlantic salmon steaks (left) and middle cut

Pink salmon *(Oncorhynchus gorbuscha)*

The smallest members of the Pacific salmon family, these have pale silver skins, with large black spots on the back and tail, and smaller scales. During the spawning season, cocks and hens become greenish brown in colour. They have pale pink flesh, which is widely used for canning. The average pink salmon weighs around 1.8kg/4lb.

Masu salmon *(Oncorhynchus masou)*

This type of Pacific salmon is mainly found off the coast of northern Japan. It is a popular game fish, but in recent years stocks have dwindled due to environmental degradation of the rivers where the fish spawn. The flesh of masu salmon is of excellent quality and this, together with the rarity value, makes it an expensive buy.

Nutrition

Salmon is a valuable protein food. It is rich in omega-3 fatty acids, which lower blood triglycerides and cholesterol levels, keeping the heart healthy, and is a good source of Vitamin A and the B-group vitamins. Farmed salmon is fatter than wild salmon, and delivers more omega-3. Smoked salmon is less nutritious, as the smoking process introduces salt and reduces nutrient levels.

CANNED SALMON

This tastes nothing like fresh salmon, and has a different texture, but it is a richer source of calcium because the bones soften during the canning process and can be eaten. Several grades are available, from the cheapest pink salmon to the best quality wild red Alaskan fish. The latter has a better flavour and texture, but pink salmon delivers higher omega-3 values. Use for mousses, quiches and fish cakes.

SMOKED SALMON

The best smoked salmon tastes so good that it would be easy to dedicate an entire cookbook to it. Smoked salmon is made by brining the fish, then dry curing it in sugar with flavourings such as whisky or molasses, and smoking it over oak or other wood chips. Cold smoking involves curing the salmon at a temperature of less than 33°C/91°F and does not actually cook the fish. For hot smoking, the temperature is 70–80°C/158–176°F and the fish is smoked and cooked simultaneously.

Depending on the strength of the cure, the type of wood chip used and the smoking time, the colour can be anything from pale pink to deep red. The quality of smoked salmon varies enormously. Avoid very cheap smoked salmon as it is likely to be thickly cut and so heavily smoked that the delicate flavour is all but overwhelmed. Good smoked salmon should always be moist and succulent.

Right: Smoked salmon

BUYING <u>AND</u> STORING SALMON

When buying salmon, whether you are choosing a whole fish for a special celebration or just buying steaks for a family supper, it pays to buy from a reputable supplier who knows his product. It is surprising how many fishmongers say they don't like fish. If that's the case, shop elsewhere, for an enthusiast is far more likely to take care when buying his fish. The ideal supplier receives daily deliveries of fish, which are kept cold on a bed of regularly replenished crushed ice or in a refrigerated cabinet. Supermarkets can be a good source of salmon. Most develop good relationships with their own suppliers, and are well aware of how important it is to have well trained, helpful staff to advise their customers.

BUYING WHOLE SALMON

Look for a fish that has shiny skin and scales that are firmly attached. The skin should feel cold and firm, and should spring back when lightly pressed. If the indentation remains, the fish is not perfectly fresh. The eyes should be clear and slightly bulbous. Cloudy or sunken eyes are a sign that the fish has been badly handled or is old. The gills should always be bright pink, not a dull brown.

Smell can also be a good indication of freshness. There should be barely any odour except perhaps the faintest aroma of riverweed.

Serving a whole salmon is inevitably a treat, so it makes sense to buy the best you can afford. Wild salmon will be considerably more expensive than farmed, but the taste will be its own reward. Order the fish in good time from your supplier, so that he can obtain it on the day required. Given notice, a good fishmonger will gut, clean and scale the fish, and will also fillet it, if that is what you want. Ask him for the trimmings, as these can be used to make fish stock.

BUYING PORTIONS

Salmon steaks, fillets or cutlets are a good buy. Salmon portions take little time to cook and can be prepared in many different ways, whether steamed, grilled (broiled), fried or baked. One of the most delicious ways of cooking salmon steaks is on a ridged grill (broiling) pan or griddle, with a little butter and oil, a dash of Tabasco and a squeeze of fresh lemon juice. As with whole salmon, buy portions on the

Below: Salmon steaks

day you plan to cook them. Although it is true that fish can be kept chilled for up to two days before being eaten, valuable nutrients will be lost if it is left to languish in the refrigerator.

SUSHI

If you are buying salmon to use raw in sushi or sashimi, the advice given about freshness is doubly important. It is vital that you can rely on your supplier to obtain the best possible fish, and for that reason it is better to order the fish in advance. Ask for a chunk from a large salmon, rather than ready-cut steaks. In Japan, fresh salmon is not used for sushi because of the risk of parasite infestation. Smoked salmon is sometimes used instead.

QUANTITIES

Allow about 175g/6oz fish fillet, cutlets or steaks for serving as a main course. There is a lot of wastage on a whole fish, so allow at least 300g/11oz per person when buying fish in this way.

STORING

It is a good idea to put salmon straight into a chiller bag when you buy it, and transfer it to the coldest part of your refrigerator as soon as you get home. If you have a meat keeper, use that for storage, but make sure that the salmon is very well wrapped, so it does not taint anything else in the refrigerator.

FREEZING

Salmon tastes best fresh, but it is sometimes not practical to cook it straight away. In that case, it is better to freeze it. Unlike some more delicate fish, salmon freezes quite well, retaining much of the original texture and taste. If you buy salmon ready-frozen, make sure it comes from a reputable supplier with a rapid turnover. Avoid freezing salmon for more than 1 month, and thaw it gradually, overnight in the refrigerator if possible. If defrosting in the microwave, separate pieces as soon as possible without tearing the flesh. Remove from the microwave when still slightly icy; if fish is thawed too much it will start to dry out.

PREPARING SALMON

Many fish suppliers will prepare fresh fish for you on request, but it is not difficult to do at home, given a sharp filleting knife and a little dexterity.

SCALING

If a salmon is going to be cooked whole, and you intend removing the skin before or after cooking it, there is no need to scale it. Scaling is essential if the salmon is to be cut into portions. The supplier will do this for you if you ask him, but if doing the job yourself, remove the fins before you start, as they can be a source of bacteria, and are likely to get in the way when you are descaling the fish. Work in the kitchen sink, to contain the scales, and so that you have access to running water.

1 Wash the whole salmon under cold water. Cut off the three fins on the underbelly, from the head to the tail, then turn the fish over and remove the dorsal fins on the back. Be careful when doing this as fins can be sharp.

2 Using a cloth to hold the fish by the tail, use a fish scaler or the back of a large cook's knife to remove the scales, working from the tail to the head. Rinse the fish and repeat the process as many times as necessary.

GUTTING/CLEANING AND BONING

You may prefer to ask your fish supplier to do this part of the preparation for you because it is a messy job. If you are doing it yourself, work on a stable work surface, and rest the fish on several thicknesses of newspaper topped with a large sheet of greaseproof (waxed) paper. Always make sure you dispose of the fish innards by wrapping them securely and removing them to an outside bin.

If you intend to serve the salmon whole, with the head on, you will need to clean it through the gills. This is slightly trickier than cleaning it by slicing through the belly, but it will preserve the appearance of the fish.

Whichever method of cleaning you choose, it is important to completely remove the gills, which would give an unpleasant, bitter taste if left on. Do this by lifting up the gill flaps, which are located on either side of the head of the fish. Push out the frilly gills and use a sharp knife to cut them off at the back of the head, under the jawbone.

Whether you are planning to cook a whole fish or to divide it into separate pieces, it will then be necessary to remove the backbone and pin bones.

Cleaning through the belly

Make sure you have your work surface well covered before you start. Use a sharp, sturdy knife, such as a filleting knife, which will allow you to make firm, smooth cuts through the fish.

1 Starting at the site of the anal fin at the tail end of the salmon, slit open the belly from tail to head, using a short, sharp filleting knife. Try to work with one clean stroke, rather than several jagged movements.

2 Carefully pull out the salmon innards, severing them at the throat and tail if necessary. Remove the gills and use a knife to scrape out the cavity, removing any blood vessels adjacent to the backbone. If left, these could impart a bitter taste when the salmon is cooked. Wash the cavity carefully with cold running water, then carefully pat the salmon dry with kitchen paper. Double wrap the innards, then put them in a sealed plastic bag in the outside bin.

Essential equipment

If you plan to prepare your own whole fish at home, it is important to make sure you that have all the necessary tools to hand. Cleaning, boning and filleting fish is relatively straightforward once you know the necessary techniques, but trying to do it without the right equipment will make your task more difficult. Fortunately, these are not unusual or expensive items.

Fish scaler The best way to remove scales from salmon skin is with a fish scaler. Brushing the back and sides of the fish with this handy utensil will get rid of scales quickly and easily.

Chef's knife A large heavy knife is invaluable for cutting whole salmon into steaks and cutlets.

Filleting knife For skinning and filleting salmon, use a flexible, long-bladed knife. Sharpen it before you start work on the fish to make sure it cuts cleanly and evenly through fish skin and flesh.

Kitchen scissors Sharp scissors with serrated edges will make short work of removing fish fins and tails.

Cleaning through the gills

This method preserves the appearance of the fish, and this is important if you plan to serve the fish whole. Make sure you have your work surface well covered before you start. Use a sharp, flexible knife, such as a filleting knife, which will allow you to make firm, smooth cuts through the flesh. Remove the gills after cleaning the fish, otherwise they will give the meat a bitter and unpleasant taste.

1 Lay the salmon on its side. Using scissors or a sharp filleting knife, make an incision in the belly, near the tail end of the fish. Locate the end of the innards with your fingertips, and cut through to separate them from the fish.

2 Using a sharp filleting knife, cut through the bone at the head of the fish, under the lower jaw. Open up the gill flaps, then insert your fingers into the cavity and gently pull out the innards. These should come away through the gill flaps, to leave the belly intact. Remove the gills.

3 Wash the cavity in running water and pat dry with kitchen paper. Double wrap the innards and put them in a sealed plastic bag in the outside bin.

Boning via the belly

If you intend stuffing the salmon and serving it whole – which is a particularly delicious way to cook salmon on the barbecue – you will need to remove the backbone. This is less difficult than it sounds. The secret is to neatly cut away the flesh so that the bones can be pulled away easily. You will need a razor-sharp filleting knife and a pair of kitchen tweezers, which are necessary to remove the small pin bones.

1 Having cleaned the salmon through the belly, place it belly up. Holding a filleting knife with the blade pointing up, and starting from the tail end, slice between the rib bones and the flesh on one side so that you free the ribs.

2 Turn the knife over and finish the job on this side by sliding the blade down the ribs to the backbone, gradually working the ribs free of the flesh. Repeat on the other side. Using sharp scissors, cut out the backbone so you can remove it with the ribs.

3 Use tweezers to remove any stray pin bones. The best way to locate these tiny bones is to feel carefully along the length of the belly with your fingertips. The cavity is now ready for stuffing.

Boning a salmon steak

Salmon cutlets or bone-in steaks are often cheaper to buy than fillets but the bone can be removed quite easily. This will give a strip of fish that can be cooked as it is or folded back into the steak shape and tied neatly for frying.

1 Insert a sharp, thin-bladed knife into the salmon cutlet at the top of the bone. Cut around the bone, staying as close to it as possible, until you reach the centre of the V-shape of the cutlet. Try to work in one smooth movement.

2 Repeat on the other side of the cutlet to free the bone completely. Gently pull out the bone. Skin the fish if you want to make it more manageable.

3 To keep the steak shape, fold the flesh and tie it neatly with string (twine).

FILLETING SALMON

If you've never filleted a round fish before, salmon is a good one to start with, as its large robust size makes the job relatively easy.

1 If the salmon has been cleaned through the belly, place it on its side and make a diagonal cut around the head, behind the gill flap. If it was cleaned through the gills, this cut may already have been made.

2 Slice through the skin from the gill down the middle of the back, holding the knife flat. Keep the knife on top of the backbone and slice the flesh away from the ribs in one piece, using long even strokes and leaving as little flesh on the ribs as possible. For a salmon cleaned through the gills, you will first need to make a cut from the gills along the middle of the belly.

Filleting fish

One advantage of filleting salmon yourself is that you are left with the head and bones for making your own fish stock. Wash the head thoroughly and remove the gills before using them for stock.

3 When the first fillet, on one side of the fish, has been removed, turn the salmon over and cut away the second fillet in the same way. Remove any pin bones with tweezers. Use the bones and trimmings for fish stock, if you like, but not the bitter gills.

SKINNING A SALMON FILLET

Round fish fillets such as salmon are skinned in exactly the same way as flat fish such as hake and skate.

1 Lay the fillet skin side down with the tail towards you. Dip your fingers in a little salt to stop them slipping and grip the tail. Angle the knife towards the skin.

2 With a sawing action, cut along the length of the fillet from the tail to the head, folding the flesh forwards as you go and keeping the skin taut.

Cutting salmon escalopes

Escalopes (US scallops) are thin pieces of boneless meat or fish, which are sometimes coated in egg and breadcrumbs before being fried. To cut salmon escalopes, skin a salmon fillet, then, holding the fillet down with your hand, use a large knife to cut the piece diagonally into thin slices. The blade should be almost flat. Hold it at enough of an angle to obtain slices about 1cm/$\frac{1}{2}$in thick. These will cook very quickly.

PREPARING FILLETS FOR COOKING

Salmon fillets can be cooked whole and flat, rolled and secured with a cocktail stick or cut into cubes.

1 If you are cooking the fillets whole, trim them with a sharp knife, cutting off very thin flaps of fish along the edges.

2 To cube a skinned salmon fillet, cut along the length of the fillet, making strips of the desired width. Then cut each strip across into cubes.

3 To roll a fillet, roll the head end towards the tail and tuck the tail underneath. Secure with a cocktail stick (toothpick).

COOKING SALMON

Despite being quite a substantial, meaty fish, salmon cooks quickly. It can be prepared in a wide variety of ways, from poaching to pan-frying, grilling (broiling) to baking and braising. It will emerge from a microwave beautifully moist and full of flavour and can be steamed or smoked with equal success.

Court-bouillon

This stock, which is flavoured with white wine and aromatics, is perfect for poaching salmon. Salt should be added only after cooking the salmon, as it can cause the flesh to stiffen. The recipe makes about 1 litre/ 1³/4 pints/4 cups.

1 Slice 1 small onion, 2 carrots and the white part of 1 large leek. Put the vegetables in a pan.

2 Add 2 fresh parsley stalks, 2 bay leaves, 2 lemon slices, 300ml/ ¹/2 pint/1¹/4 cups dry white wine and 90ml/6 tbsp white wine vinegar. Sprinkle in a few white peppercorns. Add 1 litre/1³/4 pints/4 cups water. Bring to the boil, lower the heat and simmer for 20 minutes. Strain and leave to cool before using.

Whichever method you choose, it is vital to avoid overcooking salmon. In some circles it is served when the flesh still has a ruby tint, but most people prefer salmon that has just turned opaque. Ideally, the fish should finish cooking on the way to the table, so that when it is touched with the fork, the flesh separates easily into meltingly tender flakes.

It is not possible to give precise timings for cooking salmon, since factors such as the thickness of the fish, the cooking method used and the temperature will all come into play. To ensure that the salmon cooks evenly, remove it from the refrigerator at least 30 minutes before cooking.

Salmon is cooked when its internal temperature is around 63°C/145°F, but rather than employ a meat thermometer, which is quite a specialist piece of kitchen equipment, it is best to use a visual check. Gently insert a small sharp knife into the centre of the fish and part the flesh. It should be no longer translucent and should have begun to ease away from the bone. For large pieces of salmon, it may be simpler to press a fork into the thickest part. If the prongs sink into the flesh, meeting only slight resistance near the bone, the salmon is cooked.

POACHING

This is the classic way of cooking salmon. The fish is cooked gently in either water, fish stock or an aromatic court-bouillon, and this ensures that the maximum flavour is retained.

Whole salmon

Use a fish kettle to poach whole salmon. If you do not have a fish kettle you could try to hire one from a local kitchen store, if they offer this service. It is a good idea to measure the length of your fish kettle before you shop for your fish. There's nothing more irritating than bringing home a salmon only to find it will not fit your kettle. If you are not able to obtain a fish kettle, a whole salmon can be wrapped in foil and cooked in the oven. Use the extra-large foil, sometimes known as turkey foil.

Using a fish kettle

1 Remove the metal insert from the fish kettle and place the salmon on this. Lower the salmon into the kettle. Now pour over cold court-bouillon, fish stock or water to cover the fish.

2 Add a few fresh herbs, such as parsley, dill or tarragon. Slices of lemon can be laid on top of the salmon.

3 Cover the fish with buttered baking parchment, place the pan over a medium heat and heat slowly until the water just begins to tremble. Simmer until the flesh is just opaque. If you plan to serve the salmon cold, simmer it for only 5 minutes, then remove the kettle from the heat and set it aside without lifting the lid. By the time the poaching liquid has cooled, the salmon will be perfectly cooked.

Butter sauce for poached fish

Poached fish needs very little enhancement other than a simple sauce that has been made from the poaching liquid itself.

1 Remove the cooked fish from the poaching liquid and keep it hot while you make the sauce.

2 Strain the poaching liquid into a pan and place it over a medium heat. Simmer gently until the liquid has reduced by half.

3 Whisk in some cold diced butter or a little double (heavy) cream to make a smooth, velvety sauce. Season with salt and black papper. Pour the sauce over the fish and serve.

Cooking whole salmon in foil

If you do not have a fish kettle, a whole salmon can be baked in the oven. Have ready a large piece of strong foil. Brush on 15ml/1 tbsp oil. Place the salmon on the foil and tuck some lemon slices inside the cavity. Place more lemon slices on top. Wrap the salmon loosely but securely in the foil and support in a roasting pan. Bake in a preheated oven at 150ºC/300ºF/Gas 2 for 10–15 minutes per 450g/1lb if under 2.3kg/5lb or 8 minutes per 450g/1lb if over that weight. Check the salmon frequently towards the end of cooking as timings will vary, depending on your oven and the thickness of the fish. If the salmon is very large, it may be simpler to cook it in sections, then reassemble it for serving. Clever garnishing can cover any joins.

Salmon portions

A large piece of salmon can be cooked in a pan, following the method for poaching in a fish kettle. Small portions are best poached in a dish that is large enough to hold them in a single layer.

1 Place the salmon portions in a shallow flameproof dish. Pour over court-bouillon, light fish stock or water.

2 Cover the fish with buttered baking parchment. Bring the liquid slowly to simmering point. By this time, thin portions may be cooked. Lower the heat, cover and poach thicker portions for 5–10 minutes more, until opaque.

Using the dishwasher

Many cooks claim that the best way to poach salmon is in the dishwasher. The suggested technique involves wrapping the fish in several layers of foil, placing it on the top shelf of the thoroughly clean machine, and then running the dishwasher through the hottest cycle – without detergent, of course. While this might work if the salmon is relatively small and the dishwasher offers an extra-long hot cycle, a test in a standard dishwasher was unsuccessful. The salmon was beautifully moist, but only the thinnest parts were cooked.

Fish stock

It is easy and economical to make fish stock. For 1 litre/1³/4 pints/ 4 cups stock you will need about 1kg/2¹/4lb white fish bones and trimmings from the fishmonger. Do not leave the stock simmering on the stove – after 20 minutes the flavour will deteriorate.

1 Wash any fish heads thoroughly and remove the gills, which would make the stock bitter. Chop the heads and bones if necessary. Put them in a large pan.

2 Slice the white part of 1 leek or ¹/2 fennel bulb. Chop 1 onion and 1 celery stick. Add to the fish heads and bones in the pan.

3 Pour in 150ml/¹/4 pint/²/3 cup dry white wine and 1 litre/1³/4 pints/ 4 cups water. Add 6 white peppercorns and a bouquet garni. Bring to the boil.

4 Lower the heat and simmer for 20 minutes. Remove from the heat, strain through a sieve lined with muslin (cheesecloth) and cool.

BAKING AND BRAISING

If you want to cook salmon slowly along with other vegetables and flavourings, baking and braising are ideal. To ensure the fish cooks evenly, take it out of the refrigerator 30 minutes before cooking. Aim to undercook the fish as the texture will be dry and it will lose its flavour if it is allowed to cook for too long. You can give it a little extra cooking if necessary.

Baking fillets

Salmon steaks, fillets and cutlets can all be baked in the oven. Check the fish frequently because cooking times will vary, depending on the cut and size of the fish, the method of baking and the effectiveness of your oven.

Chunky salmon steaks and cutlets are perfect for baking in a roasting pan in the oven. The temperature should be no higher than 200°C/400°F/Gas 6. Keep the fish moist by coating it in a sauce or olive oil or by wrapping it in foil.

Another way of retaining maximum moisture is to cook the salmon *en papillote*, which means in a foil or paper parcel. Add a couple of slices of lemon and some fresh dill or other herbs. No additional fat is needed, so this is a very healthy option.

Braising fillets

This is an excellent cooking method for larger salmon fillets. Adding the stock helps to keep the fish beautifully moist.

1 Butter a flameproof dish and arrange a thick bed of thinly sliced or shredded vegetables on the base. A mixture of leeks, fennel and carrots works well.

2 Place the fish on top of the vegetables and pour on enough dry white wine, court-bouillon or light fish stock to come nearly halfway up the fish.

3 Sprinkle over 15ml/1 tbsp chopped fresh herbs, then cover with buttered baking parchment and set over a high heat. Bring the liquid to the boil. Braise over a low heat on top of the stove or in an oven preheated to 180°C/350°F/Gas 4 for 10–15 minutes.

FRYING

Pan-frying is particularly well-suited to salmon because the flesh is robust and the flavours will not be diminished. Stir-frying in a wok is just as tasty, but it uses less oil and makes a healthier alternative to pan-frying.

Pan-frying

Salmon tastes absolutely delicious when lightly pan-fried in butter, fruity olive oil or a mixture of the two.

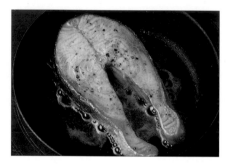

Heat the fat in the pan. When it is very hot, add the fish and seal briefly on both sides. Lower the heat and cook the fish gently until done. If the pieces of fish are large or the recipe is more complex it may be necessary to finish cooking the fish in an oven preheated to 180°C/350°F/Gas 4.

Searing

This method gives the best results with thick fillets of salmon, with the skin on.

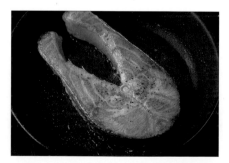

Smear the base of a frying pan or griddle with a little oil and heat until smoking. Brush both sides of the salmon with oil and put into the hot pan, skin down. Sear for 2 minutes, until the skin is golden brown, then turn the fish over and cook the other side.

Stir-frying

This quick Asian cooking style is perfect for many types of fish. Strips of salmon taste delicious stir-fried with thinly sliced spring onions (scallions) and slices of baby fennel. Stir-fry the vegetables briefly in hot oil, then add the salmon strips, lightly moistened with soy sauce, and stir-fry for 1–2 minutes until cooked but still in one piece.

1 Cut the salmon fillets into bitesize strips. Toss in a little cornflour (cornstarch) to prevent them falling apart as they cook in the oil.

2 Heat vegetable oil in a wok or frying pan over a very high heat. Add the pieces of salmon to the wok and stir-fry for a few moments. You may need to cook the pieces in batches, depending on the amount of fish you wish to cook and the size of your wok.

3 As each batch of salmon pieces is cooked, remove them from the wok and keep warm as you cook further batches.

Deep-frying salmon

Salmon pieces are seldom deep-fried in the way that cod or haddock are. The reason for this is not so much because salmon is not suitable for deep-frying – quite the opposite in fact, because its firm, meaty flesh is perfectly capable of holding its shape – but because frying impairs the special flavour and texture. The exception is when thin strips of salmon fillet are transformed into goujons by coating them in milk and flour and deep-frying them in oil.

Goujons of salmon

Crisp on the outside and succulent and tender within, salmon goujons taste wonderful served with a creamy dipping sauce.

SERVES 4

INGREDIENTS
  1 salmon fillet, about 350g/12oz
  120ml/4fl oz/$^1/_2$ cup milk
  50g/2oz/$^1/_2$ cup plain
    (all-purpose) flour
  salt and ground black pepper
  oil, for deep-frying

1 Skin the salmon fillet and cut it into 7.5 x 2.5cm/3 x 1in strips. Pour the milk into a shallow bowl. Season the flour and spread it out in a separate shallow bowl.

2 Dip the salmon strips into the milk, then into the seasoned flour. Shake off the excess flour.

3 Heat the oil for deep-frying to about 185°C/360°F or until a small cube of bread dropped into the oil turns brown in 30 seconds.

4 Lower the salmon strips into the oil, adding four or five at a time. Fry for 3 minutes, turning them occasionally with a slotted spoon, until they have risen to the surface and are golden brown in colour.

5 Lift out each goujon in turn with a slotted spoon and drain on kitchen paper. Keep hot in the oven while you cook successive batches.

ON THE BARBECUE

This is a very good way of cooking salmon. Either marinate steaks or thick fillets (with the skin on) for at least an hour before cooking, or brush them with vegetable or olive oil just before cooking over medium coals. If you are entertaining in large numbers, you could cook a whole salmon on the barbecue. If you have a hinged grill, put the prepared salmon directly on the grill. Otherwise, wrap the salmon in a large sheet of foil. A 2.25kg/5lb salmon will take from 45 minutes to 1 hour to cook, depending on the heat of the coals and whether or not the fish is wrapped in foil.

Marinate the salmon pieces in a mixture of olive oil and lemon juice, making deep slashes in the side of the fish so that the marinade penetrates right the way through and the heat is conducted evenly through the flesh. Leave the fish in the refrigerator to marinate for a minimum of 1 hour.

A ridged griddle set on the barbecue is good for cooking salmon. Grease it lightly with oil to prevent the skin of the salmon from sticking – an oil spray will give the best coverage with the least amount of oil.

GRILLING

When grilling (broiling) salmon steaks or fillets, high heat should be used initially, to seal in the fish juices. Regardless of the recipe, the fish will always benefit from being marinated in a mixture of oil and lemon juice before being grilled. Brush the grill (broiling) rack with oil, and if the fish has not been marinated, brush it with oil too. Turn thick salmon steaks or fillets over once the surface is sealed, and grill the other side until cooked through. Thin fillets will not need to be turned. Cubes of salmon make excellent kebabs.

MICROWAVING

Salmon cooks well in the microwave. Always cover the fish with microwave clear film (plastic wrap). Cook on full power (100 per cent) for the time recommended in your handbook, then give it a resting period so that it finishes cooking by residual heat. As a general guide, thick fillets, steaks and cutlets will take 4–5 minutes and should be left to stand for a further 5 minutes.

Cook salmon fillets in a single layer in a microwave dish. Put thinner parts towards the centre, or tuck a thin end underneath a thicker portion.

ROASTING

Thick pieces of salmon can be roasted successfully. As with grilling it is a good idea to marinate the fish in oil and lemon juice beforehand. Preheat the oven to 230°C/450°F/Gas 8, with the roasting pan inside. Add the pieces of fish, skin side down, to the hot pan. This will sear the skin and help to retain the juices. Fillets will take about 10–12 minutes; steaks 15–20 minutes.

STEAMING

This is the healthiest way of cooking salmon, since no extra fat is required and nutrients are retained, and the steaming process enhances the natural flavour. Salmon cooks quickly this way, but even if you overcook it the fish will retain its shape and remain moist.

1 Half-fill the base pan of a metal steamer with water and bring to the boil. Lower the steamer insert into the base, making sure that it stands well clear of the boiling water.

2 Place the fish in a single layer in the steamer basket, leaving room for the steam to circulate freely. Add fresh herbs with the salmon if you like.

3 Lay a sheet of greaseproof (waxed) paper loosely over the surface of the fish, then cover the pan tightly with a lid or foil. Steam until the fish is just cooked through.

4 Salmon cooks very quickly in a steamer, but take care that the level of the water does not fall too low, or the base of the pan will burn. Check once or twice during cooking and keep a kettle of boiling water on hand to top it up if necessary.

Alternative steaming methods

There are plenty of purpose-made steamers on the market, ranging from the hugely expensive stainless steel models to modest Chinese bamboo baskets. However, you can easily improvise with a large pan, any perforated container, such as a colander or sieve, and some foil. It is important to make sure that the pan is large enough to hold several inches of water.

Whatever the type of steamer you use, remember that the golden rule of steaming is not to allow the boiling liquid to touch the steamer basket or the salmon inside it. This would mean that the fish was boiling in water, and all of its nutritional value would be lost.

A Chinese bamboo steamer is ideal for steaming salmon. Arrange the fish, skin side up, on a bed of aromatic flavourings, such as lemon slices and fresh herbs, or on finely shredded vegetables. Place the steamer in a wok or on top of a large pan of boiling water and steam until the fish is cooked.

SMOKING

Salmon can be smoked at home, either in a small domestic smoker or a kettle barbecue. Follow the instructions in your handbook. In the kitchen, the Chinese method of tea smoking works well, but it helps if you have an extractor fan to remove excess smoke.

1 Line a wok with foil and sprinkle in 30ml/2 tbsp each of raw long grain rice, sugar and aromatic tea leaves.

2 Place a wire rack on the wok and add the salmon fillets in a single layer.

3 Cover the wok with a lid or more foil and cook over a very high heat until smoke appears. Lower the heat slightly (some smoke should still escape from the wok) and cook for 10–15 minutes more until the fish is done.

RAW SALMON

Very fresh salmon that has been bought from a reliable fishmonger or supplier can also be served raw, as smoked salmon, sushi or sashimi, or brined to make the delectable Scandinavian speciality known as gravlax.

Home-cured gravlax

Although almost every supermarket sells ready-cured gravlax, it is very easy to prepare at home. For eight people you will need 1–1.2kg/2¼–2½lb of absolutely fresh middle-cut salmon that has already been boned and cut lengthways into two fillets.

1 For the curing mix, mix 30ml/2 tbsp coarse sea salt, 30ml/2 tbsp caster (superfine) sugar, 15–30ml/1–2 tbsp crushed black peppercorns and a handful of chopped fresh dill.

2 Lay one salmon fillet skin side down in a non-metallic dish. Cover with a generous layer of the curing mix. Lay the second fillet on top, skin side up, and sprinkle on the remaining mix. Cover with clear film (plastic wrap).

3 Place a wooden board slightly larger than the non-metallic dish on top of the salmon and weigh it down with heavy cans or weights.

4 Leave in the refrigerator for at least 72 hours, turning the salmon every 12 hours and basting it with the juices that have oozed out. To serve, slice on the diagonal, a little thicker than you would for smoked salmon.

Above: Gravlax

Flavourings for salmon

Salmon is a hugely versatile fish and it works well with a range of flavourings. The following can be used to adapt your own recipes or some of those featured in this book.

Companion flavourings Salmon has a natural affinity for fresh-tasting herbs like parsley, chervil and tarragon. Dill, with its aniseed flavour, is a great favourite, and is essential in the Swedish sugar-and-salt-cured dish, gravlax. Citrus flavourings like lemon and lime are obvious choices, but try lemon grass for a more subtle taste, or that little used but delicious herb, sorrel.

Fusion flavours Aromatics like ginger and galangal go well with salmon, as does fresh garlic. Spring onions (scallions), leeks and shallots are also suitable, and are especially good to use in marinades and sauces. Fennel has a similar flavour to dill, the herb that works so well with salmon, so try roasting salmon on a bed of thinly sliced fennel, with the fronds chopped and added to a sauce or used as a garnish.

Nuts It is well known that almonds go well with trout, but you can try them with salmon too. Brown them in butter or use them in a stuffing for whole salmon. Other nuts you could try include hazelnuts, pine nuts, pistachios and macadamias.

A splash of wine Dry white wine is the obvious choice of alcohol for flavouring salmon, and it is often mixed with court-bouillon. The Mediterranean aperitif drinks pastis and ouzo are also appropriate, as they have the slightly aniseed flavour that balances the oiliness of the fish. For warmer flavours, try rice wine such as sake or mirin. Ginger wine could also be used, but don't overdo it, as its powerful flavour could be a bit overwhelming. For an alcohol-free cooking medium, use a good homemade court-bouillon or fish stock or coconut milk.

SOUPS AND APPETIZERS

One of the many attributes of salmon, aside from its excellent flavour and texture, is the delicate pink colour, and nowhere is this capitalized on more effectively than in the preparation of soups and appetizers. Salmon chowder, for instance, looks so delicious in the bowl that it would seem a shame to disturb it, were it not for the wonderful aroma that rises from the surface. Mousses, terrines and pâtés are just as pretty, especially when smoked salmon is used as a wrapper or garnish. The most dramatic effects, however, come from Japanese kitchens, where very fresh raw salmon is enclosed in jet-black yaki-nori to make superb sushi.

SALMON CHOWDER

DILL IS THE PERFECT PARTNER FOR SALMON IN THIS CREAMY SOUP FROM THE USA. IT TAKES ITS INSPIRATION FROM THE SATISFYING SOUPS THAT ARE TYPICAL OF THE EASTERN SEABOARD OF THE UNITED STATES AND IS BEST SERVED IMMEDIATELY AFTER COOKING, WHEN THE SALMON IS JUST TENDER.

SERVES 4

INGREDIENTS
   20g/¾oz/1½ tbsp butter
   1 onion, finely chopped
   1 leek, finely chopped
   1 small fennel bulb, finely chopped
   25g/1oz/¼ cup plain
      (all-purpose) flour
   1.75 litres/3 pints/7 cups fish stock
   2 medium potatoes, cut in
      1cm/½in cubes
   450g/1lb salmon fillet, skinned and
      cut into 2cm/¾in cubes
   175ml/6fl oz/¾ cup milk
   120ml/4fl oz/½ cup whipping cream
   30ml/2 tbsp chopped fresh dill
   salt and ground black pepper

1 Melt the butter in a large pan. Add the onion, leek and chopped fennel and cook for 6 minutes until softened.

2 Stir in the flour. Reduce the heat to low and cook for 3 minutes, stirring occasionally with a wooden spoon.

3 Add the fish stock and potatoes to the mixture in the pan. Season with a little salt and ground black pepper. Bring to the boil, then reduce the heat, cover and simmer gently for about 20 minutes or until the potatoes are tender when tested with a fork.

4 Add the cubed salmon fillet and simmer gently for 3–5 minutes until it is just cooked.

5 Stir the milk, cream, and chopped dill into the contents of the pan. Cook until just warmed through, stirring occasionally, but do not allow to boil. Adjust the seasoning to taste, then ladle into warmed soup bowls to serve.

CUCUMBER <u>AND</u> YOGURT SOUP <u>WITH</u> SALSA

CHARRED SALMON FILLET BRINGS A HINT OF HEAT TO THE COOL, REFRESHING FLAVOURS OF THIS CHILLED CUCUMBER AND YOGURT SOUP. ATTRACTIVE, DELICIOUS AND BEAUTIFULLY LIGHT, IT MAKES THE PERFECT OPENER FOR AN ALFRESCO MEAL.

SERVES 4

INGREDIENTS

3 medium cucumbers
300ml/½ pint/1¼ cups Greek
  (US strained plain) yogurt
250ml/8fl oz/1 cup vegetable
  stock, chilled
120ml/4fl oz/½ cup
  crème fraîche
15ml/1 tbsp chopped
  fresh chervil
15ml/1 tbsp chopped
  fresh chives
15ml/1 tbsp chopped fresh
  flat-leaf parsley
1 small fresh red chilli, seeded and
  very finely chopped
a little oil, for brushing
225g/8oz salmon fillet, skinned and
  cut into eight thin slices
salt and ground black pepper
fresh chervil or chives, to garnish

4 Brush a griddle or frying pan with oil and heat until very hot. Add the salmon slices and sear them for 1–2 minutes, then turn over carefully and sear the other side until tender and charred.

5 Ladle the chilled soup into soup bowls. Top each portion with two slices of salmon, then pile a portion of salsa into the centre. Garnish with the chervil or chives and serve.

1 Peel two of the cucumbers and halve them lengthways. Scoop out and discard the seeds, then roughly chop the flesh. Purée the chopped flesh in a food processor or blender.

2 Add the yogurt, stock, crème fraîche, chervil, chives and seasoning, and process until smooth. Pour into a bowl, cover and chill.

3 Peel, halve and seed the remaining cucumber. Cut the flesh into small neat dice. Mix with the chopped parsley and chilli in a bowl. Cover the salsa and chill until required.

NOODLE, PAK CHOI AND SALMON RAMEN

THIS LIGHTLY SPICED JAPANESE NOODLE SOUP IS ENHANCED WITH SLICES OF SEARED FRESH SALMON AND CRISP GREEN VEGETABLES. THE DELIGHTFUL CONTRASTS IN TEXTURE AND DELICATE MIX OF COLOURS ARE ALMOST AS APPEALING AS THE DELICIOUSLY PIQUANT TASTE.

SERVES 4

INGREDIENTS

1.5 litres/2½ pints/6 cups good
   vegetable stock
2.5cm/1in piece fresh root ginger,
   finely sliced
2 garlic cloves, crushed
6 spring onions (scallions), sliced
45ml/3 tbsp soy sauce
45ml/3 tbsp sake
450g/1lb salmon fillet, skinned
5ml/1 tsp groundnut (peanut) oil
350g/12oz ramen or udon noodles
4 small heads pak choi (bok choy),
   broken into leaves
1 fresh red chilli,
   seeded and sliced
50g/2oz/1 cup beansprouts
salt and ground black pepper

1 Pour the vegetable stock into a large pan and add the ginger, garlic, and a third of the spring onions.

2 Add the soy sauce and sake. Bring the stock to the boil, then reduce the heat to a simmer and leave to cook for 30 minutes.

3 Meanwhile, carefully remove any pin bones from the salmon fillet using tweezers, then cut the salmon on the slant into 12 slices of even thickness, using a very sharp knife.

4 Brush a ridged griddle or frying pan with the groundnut oil and allow to heat until very hot. Sear the salmon slices for 1–2 minutes on each side until tender and marked by the ridges of the pan. Set aside.

COOK'S TIP
To obtain the distinctive stripes on the slices of salmon, it is important that the ridged pan or griddle is well oiled and very hot before they are added. Avoid moving the slices around once they are placed on the griddle, or the stripes will become blurred.

5 Cook the ramen or udon noodles in a large pan of boiling water for 4–5 minutes or according to the instructions on the packet. Transfer into a colander, drain well and refresh under cold running water. Drain again and set aside.

6 Strain the broth into a clean pan and season, then bring to the boil. Add the pak choi. Using a fork, twist the noodles into four nests and put these into deep bowls. Divide the salmon slices, spring onions, chilli and beansprouts among the bowls. Ladle in the broth.

CURRIED SALMON SOUP

A HINT OF MILD CURRY PASTE REALLY ENHANCES THE FLAVOUR OF THIS SOUP, WITHOUT MAKING IT TOO SPICY. GRATED CREAMED COCONUT ADDS A LUXURY TOUCH, WHILE HELPING TO AMALGAMATE THE FLAVOURS. SERVED WITH CHUNKS OF WARM BREAD, THIS MAKES A SUBSTANTIAL APPETIZER.

SERVES 4

INGREDIENTS
  50g/2oz/¼ cup butter
  2 onions, roughly chopped
  10ml/2 tsp mild curry paste
  475ml/16fl oz/2 cups water
  150ml/¼ pint/⅔ cup white wine
  300ml/½ pint/1¼ cups double
   (heavy) cream
  50g/2oz/½ cup creamed coconut,
   grated or 120ml/4fl oz/½ cup
   coconut cream
  2 potatoes, about 350g/12oz, cubed
  450g/1lb salmon fillet, skinned
   and cut into bitesize pieces
  60ml/4 tbsp chopped fresh
   flat-leaf parsley
salt and ground black pepper

1 Melt the butter in a large pan, add the onions and cook for about 3–4 minutes until beginning to soften. Stir in the curry paste. Cook for 1 minute more.

2 Add the water, wine, cream and creamed coconut or coconut cream, with seasoning. Bring to the boil, stirring until the coconut has dissolved.

3 Add the potatoes to the pan. Simmer, covered, for about 15 minutes or until they are almost tender. Do not allow them to break down into the mixture.

4 Add the fish gently so as not to break it up. Simmer for 2–3 minutes until just cooked. Add the parsley and adjust the seasoning. Serve immediately.

RICE IN GREEN TEA WITH SALMON

IN THE KYOTO REGION OF JAPAN, OFFERING THIS DISH TO GUESTS USED TO BE A POLITE WAY OF SAYING THE PARTY WAS OVER. THE GUESTS WERE EXPECTED TO DECLINE AND LEAVE IMMEDIATELY.

SERVES 4

INGREDIENTS

   150g/5oz salmon fillet
   ¼ sheet nori
   250g/9oz/1¼ cups Japanese short
     grain rice cooked as advised on
     the packet, using 350ml/12fl oz/
     1½ cups water
   15ml/1 tbsp sencha leaves
   600ml/1 pint/2½ cups water
   5ml/1 tsp wasabi paste or 5ml/1 tsp
     wasabi powder mixed with 1.5ml/
     ¼ tsp water (optional)
   20ml/4 tsp shoyu (Japanese soy sauce)
   sea salt

1 Place the salmon fillet in a bowl and cover it with salt. If the fillet is thicker than 2.5cm/1in, slice it in half and salt both halves. Leave for 30 minutes.

2 Wipe the salt off the salmon with kitchen paper and grill (broil) the fish under a preheated grill (broiler) for about 5 minutes until cooked through.

3 Using scissors, cut the nori into short, narrow strips about 20 x 5mm/ ¾ x ¼in long, or leave as long narrow strips, if you prefer.

4 Remove the skin and any bones from the salmon, then flake the fish.

5 If the cooked rice is warm, put equal amounts into individual rice bowls or soup bowls. If the rice is cold, put it in a sieve (strainer) and pour hot water from a kettle over it to warm it up. Drain and pour into the bowls. Place the salmon pieces on top of the rice.

6 Put the sencha leaves in a teapot. Bring the water to the boil, remove from the heat and leave to cool slightly. Pour into the teapot and wait for 45 seconds.

7 Strain the tea gently and evenly over the top of the rice and salmon. Add some nori and wasabi, if using, to the top of each portion of rice, then trickle shoyu over and serve.

COOK'S TIP
Sencha are fine green tea leaves available from Japanese food stores and shops or markets selling specialist teas.

MARINATED SALMON WITH AVOCADO

USE ONLY THE FRESHEST OF SALMON FOR THIS DELICIOUS SALAD. THE MARINADE OF LEMON AND DASHI-KONBU "COOKS" THE SALMON, WHICH IS SERVED WITH AVOCADO, ALMONDS AND SALAD LEAVES.

SERVES 4

INGREDIENTS
 250g/9oz very fresh salmon tail,
  skinned and filleted
 juice of 1 lemon
 10cm/4in dashi-konbu (dried kelp
  seaweed), wiped with a damp cloth
  and cut into 4 strips
 1 ripe avocado
 4 shiso leaves, stalks removed and
  cut in half lengthways
 about 115g/4oz mixed leaves such
  as lamb's lettuce, frisée or rocket
  (arugula)
 45ml/3 tbsp flaked or sliced almonds,
  toasted in a dry frying pan

For the miso mayonnaise
 90ml/6 tbsp good-quality mayonnaise
 15ml/1 tbsp shiro miso
 ground black pepper
 15ml/1 tbsp lemon juice

1 Cut the first salmon fillet in half crossways at the tail end where the fillet is not wider than 4cm/1½in. Next, cut the wider part of the fillet in half lengthways. This means the fillet from one side is cut into three. Cut the other fillet into three pieces in the same way.

COOK'S TIP
Shiro miso, fermented soya bean paste, can be bought at Japanese food stores and from online suppliers.

2 Pour the lemon juice and put two of the dashi-konbu pieces into a wide shallow plastic container. Lay the salmon fillets in the base and sprinkle with the rest of the dashi-konbu. Marinate for 15 minutes, then turn once and leave for 15 minutes more. Drain and pat dry with kitchen paper.

3 Holding a very sharp knife at an angle, cut the salmon into 5mm/¼in thick slices against the grain.

4 Halve the avocado and brush the cut surface with a little of the remaining salmon marinade. Remove the avocado stone (pit) and skin, then carefully slice to the same thickness as the salmon.

5 Make miso mayonnaise by mixing the mayonnaise, shiro miso and pepper in a small bowl. Spread about 5ml/1 tsp on to the back of each of the shiso leaves, then mix the remainder with the lemon juice to loosen the mayonnaise.

6 Arrange the salad on four plates. Top with the avocado, salmon, shiso leaves and almonds. Drizzle over the remaining miso mayonnaise. Serve immediately.

SMOKED FISH PLATTER <u>WITH</u> HONEY DRESSING

TROUT, SALMON AND MACKEREL FEATURE IN THIS APPETIZER — BUT ANY SMOKED FISH CAN BE USED.
ASK YOUR LOCAL FISHMONGER OR INQUIRE AT THE FISH COUNTER FOR THE BEST BUYS.

SERVES 4

INGREDIENTS
½ Charentais melon
½ cantaloupe melon
50g/2oz rocket (arugula)
75g/3oz hot-smoked trout fillets
75g/3oz smoked salmon
75g/3oz smoked mackerel
with peppercorns

For the dressing
75ml/5 tbsp extra virgin
olive oil
15ml/1 tbsp white
wine vinegar
5ml/1 tsp wholegrain mustard
5ml/1 tsp clear honey
salt and ground black pepper

COOK'S TIP
Among the more unusual types of
smoked fish available are smoked halibut
and smoked sturgeon. Smoked halibut
has translucent white flesh and this,
coupled with its delicate flavour, would
make it a good addition to the fish
platter. Smoked sturgeon would be a
real talking point at any dinner table.
A luxury fish, comparable with the finest
smoked salmon, it is best served solo,
so its rich flavour and succulent texture
can be fully appreciated.

1 Scoop out and discard all the seeds
from the Charentais and cantaloupe
melons and cut each melon into four
or eight slices, leaving the skin on.
Divide the melon slices among four
small serving plates, placing the slices
neatly to one side.

2 Add a quarter of the rocket leaves
to each plate, placing them opposite
the melon.

3 Make the honey dressing by
combining all the ingredients in a small
jug (pitcher). Add plenty of salt and
black pepper and whisk with a fork
until emulsified.

4 Divide the smoked fish into four
portions, breaking or cutting the trout
fillets and smoked salmon into bitesize
pieces. Peel the skin from the mackerel,
then break up the flesh. Arrange
the trout fillets, smoked salmon and
mackerel over the rocket and melon
on each platter. Drizzle the dressing
over and serve immediately.

FISH TERRINE

THIS COLOURFUL LAYERED TERRINE MAKES A SPECTACULAR PRESENTATION FOR A SPECIAL OCCASION. IT IS PERFECT FOR ENTERTAINING SINCE IT IS BEST MADE THE DAY BEFORE AND CHILLED OVERNIGHT.

SERVES 6 AS PART OF A BUFFET

INGREDIENTS
   450g/1lb white fish fillets, skinned
   225–275g/8–10oz thinly sliced
      smoked salmon
   2 egg whites, chilled
   1.5ml/¼ tsp each salt and
      white pepper
   pinch of freshly grated nutmeg
   250ml/8fl oz/1 cup
      whipping cream
   60g/2oz baby spinach leaves
   lemon mayonnaise, to serve

1 Cut the white fish fillets into evenly sized 2.5cm/1in pieces, removing any pin bones with tweezers as you work. Spread out the fish pieces on a plate and cover with clear film (plastic wrap). Place the plate in the freezer for about 15 minutes until the fish is very cold, but not frozen.

2 Lightly grease a 1.2 litre/2 pint/5 cup terrine or loaf tin (pan). Line the base with baking parchment, then line the base and sides of the tin with smoked salmon slices, letting them hang over the edge. Preheat the oven to 180°C/350°F/Gas 4.

3 Put the pieces of chilled fish in a food processor and whizz to a very smooth purée, stopping the machine several times to scrape down the sides.

4 Add the egg whites, one at a time, then the salt, pepper and nutmeg. With the machine running, pour in the cream through the feeder tube. Stop as soon as it is blended. (If overprocessed, the cream will thicken too much.)

5 Transfer the fish mixture to a large glass bowl. Put the spinach leaves into the food processor and process to a purée. Add one-third of the fish mixture to the spinach and process until just combined, scraping down the sides once or twice.

6 Spread half the plain fish mixture in the base of the tin and smooth it level. Spoon the green fish mixture over the top and smooth the surface, then cover with the remaining plain mixture and smooth the top.

7 Fold the overhanging pieces of salmon over the top to enclose the fish mixture. Tap the tin to settle the mixture and remove any air pockets, then cover the terrine with a double layer of foil.

8 Put the terrine in a roasting pan and pour in enough boiling water to come halfway up the sides of the terrine. Bake for about 1 hour, until a skewer inserted in the centre comes out clean. Allow to cool, wrap well and chill for 3–4 hours or overnight, until firm.

9 To serve the terrine, invert on a board and slice. Arrange slices on individual plates and serve with lemon mayonnaise.

SMOKED SALMON TERRINE WITH LEMONS

THIS MELT-IN-THE-MOUTH SMOKED SALMON TERRINE MAKES A SPECTACULAR FIRST COURSE FOR A SPECIAL DINNER. FOR THE WRAPPED LEMON HALVES YOU WILL NEED SOME MUSLIN AND RAFFIA.

SERVES 6

INGREDIENTS
  4 sheets leaf gelatine
  60ml/4 tbsp water
  400g/14oz smoked salmon, sliced
  300g/11oz/scant 1½ cups
    cream cheese
  120ml/4fl oz/½ cup crème fraîche
  30ml/2 tbsp dill mustard
  juice of 1 lime
  2 lemons, to garnish (optional)

1 Soak the gelatine in the water in a small bowl until softened. Meanwhile, line a 450g/1lb loaf tin (pan) with clear film (plastic wrap). Use some of the smoked salmon to line the tin, laying the slices widthways across the base and up the sides and leaving enough hanging over the edge to fold over the top of the filling.

2 Set aside enough of the remaining smoked salmon to make a middle layer the length of the tin. Chop the rest finely by hand or in a food processor. Take care not to over-process the salmon.

3 In a bowl, beat the cream cheese, crème fraîche and dill mustard, add the chopped salmon and mix with a rubber spatula until well combined.

4 Squeeze out the gelatine and put the sheets in a small, heavy pan. Add the lime juice. Place over a low heat until the gelatine has melted, cool slightly, then stir into the salmon mixture.

5 Spoon half the mixture into the lined tin. Lay the reserved smoked salmon slices on the mixture along the length of the tin, then spoon on the rest of the filling and smooth the top.

6 Tap the tin on the surface to expel any trapped air. Fold over the over-hanging salmon slices to cover the top. Cover the whole tin with clear film and place in the refrigerator to chill for at least 4 hours, preferably 6–8 hours.

7 If making the lemon garnish, cut one lemon in half widthways. Wrap each half in a small square of muslin (cheesecloth). Gather the muslin at the end of the lemon and tie with raffia.

8 Cut a small "V" from the side of the other lemon. Repeat at 5mm/¼in intervals. Turn out the terrine, then slice. Garnish with the muslin-wrapped lemons and lemon "leaves".

STRIPED FISH TERRINE

ROSE AND CREAM, THE DELICATE COLOURS OF SALMON AND SOLE GIVE THIS TASTY TERRINE A VERY PRETTY APPEARANCE. SERVE IT COLD OR JUST WARM, WITH A HOLLANDAISE SAUCE IF YOU LIKE.

SERVES 8

INGREDIENTS
   15ml/1 tbsp sunflower oil
   450g/1lb salmon fillet, skinned
   450g/1lb sole fillets, skinned
   3 egg whites
   105ml/7 tbsp double (heavy) cream
   15ml/1 tbsp fresh chives,
     finely chopped
   juice of 1 lemon
   115g/4oz/scant 1 cup fresh or frozen
     peas, cooked
   5ml/1 tsp chopped fresh mint leaves
   salt, ground white pepper and freshly
     grated nutmeg
   thinly sliced cucumber, salad or land
     cress and chives, to garnish

1 Grease a 1 litre/1¾ pint/4 cup loaf tin (pan) with the oil. Slice the salmon thinly; cut it and the sole into long strips, 2.5cm/1in wide. Preheat the oven to 200°C/400°F/Gas 6.

2 Line the tin neatly with alternate slices of salmon and sole, leaving the ends hanging over the edge. You should be left with about a third of the salmon and half the sole.

3 In a grease-free bowl, beat the egg whites with a pinch of salt until they form soft peaks. Purée the remaining sole in a food processor. Spoon into a large mixing bowl, season, then fold in two-thirds of the egg whites, followed by two-thirds of the cream. Put half the mixture into a second mixing bowl; stir in the finely chopped chives. Add nutmeg to the first bowl.

4 Purée the remaining salmon, scrape it into a bowl and add the lemon juice. Fold in the remaining whites and cream.

5 Purée the cooked peas with the mint. Season the mixture and spread it over the base of the fish-lined tin, smoothing the surface with a spatula. Spoon over the sole with chives mixture and spread evenly over the pea layer.

6 Spoon over the salmon mixture, then top with the sole and nutmeg mixture. Cover with the overhanging fish fillets and foil lid. Stand the tin in a roasting pan and pour in enough boiling water to come halfway up the sides.

7 Bake for 15–20 minutes, until the top fillets are just cooked and the mousse feels springy. Remove the foil, lay a wire rack over the top of the terrine and invert both rack and tin on to a lipped baking sheet to catch the cooking juices that drain out.

8 Let the tin stand for about 15 minutes, then turn the tin by inverting it on to a serving dish and lifting off the pan. Serve warm or lightly chilled, garnished with sliced cucumber, salad or land cress and chives.

SALMON AND PIKE MOUSSE

WHEN SLICED, THIS LIGHT-TEXTURED RUSSIAN MOUSSE LOAF, PATE IZ SHCHUKI, REVEALS A PRETTY LAYER OF DELICATELY PINK SALMON. FOR A TREAT OR SPECIAL OCCASION, SERVE TOPPED WITH RED SALMON ROE AND FEATHERY SPRIGS OF FRESHLY PICKED DILL.

3 Cut the pike into cubes and process in a food processor or blender until smooth. Lightly whisk the egg whites with a fork. With the motor of the food processor or blender running, slowly pour in the egg whites, then the cream through the feeder tube or lid. Finally, add the lemon rind and dill. Taste the mixture and add a little salt and pepper if you think more seasoning is needed.

4 Spoon half of the pike mixture into the loaf tin. Arrange the poached salmon strips on top, then carefully spoon in the remaining pike mixture.

5 Cover the loaf tin with foil and put in a roasting pan. Add enough boiling water to come halfway up the sides of the loaf tin. Bake for 45–50 minutes, or until firm.

SERVES 8

INGREDIENTS
  10ml/2 tsp oil
  225g/8oz salmon fillet, skinned
  600ml/1 pint/2½ cups fish stock
  finely grated rind and juice of
    ½ lemon
  900g/2lb pike fillets, skinned
  4 egg whites
  475ml/16fl oz/2 cups double
    (heavy) cream
  30ml/2 tbsp chopped fresh dill
  salt and ground black pepper
  red salmon roe or a fresh dill sprig,
    to garnish (optional)

COOK'S TIP
If you have difficulty locating pike, you can substitute turbot, sea bream or sole for the pike in this recipe.

1 Preheat the oven to 180°C/350°F/ Gas 4. Brush a 900g/2lb loaf tin (pan) with oil and line with baking parchment.

2 Cut the salmon into 5cm/2in strips. Pour the stock and lemon juice into a pan and bring to the boil, then turn off the heat. Add the salmon strips, cover and leave for 2 minutes. Remove with a slotted spoon.

6 Leave on a wire rack to cool, then chill for at least 3 hours. Invert on to a serving plate and remove the lining paper. Serve the mousse in slices. Garnish with red salmon roe or a sprig of fresh dill, if you like. A spoonful of crème fraîche could also be added.

SMOKED SALMON AND HERB ROULADE

*MAKE THE MOST OF A SMALL AMOUNT OF SMOKED SALMON BY USING IT IN THE FILLING FOR THIS
DELICATELY FLAVOURED ROULADE. MAKE THE ROULADE IN ADVANCE TO GIVE IT TIME TO COOL, BUT
DON'T PUT IT IN THE REFRIGERATOR OR IT WILL LOSE ITS LIGHT TEXTURE.*

SERVES 6–8 AS PART OF A BUFFET

INGREDIENTS
  25g/1oz/2 tbsp butter
  25g/1oz/¼ cup plain
    (all-purpose) flour
  175ml/6fl oz/¾ cup milk, warm
  3 large eggs, separated
  50g/2oz/⅔ cup freshly grated
    Parmesan cheese
  60ml/4 tbsp chopped fresh dill
  30ml/2 tbsp chopped fresh parsley
  150ml/¼ pint/⅔ cup full fat crème
    fraîche or sour cream
  115g/4oz smoked salmon
  salt and ground black pepper
  lamb's lettuce, to garnish

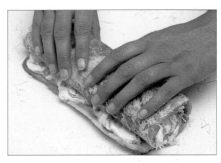

3 Coarsely chop the smoked salmon, then mix it in a bowl with the crème fraîche or sour cream and remaining chopped dill. Stir gently but thoroughly, then taste and add salt and pepper as needed.

4 Peel off the lining paper from the roulade, spread the filling evenly over the surface and roll up, then leave to firm up in a cold place. Sprinkle with the rest of the Parmesan and garnish with the lamb's lettuce.

1 Melt the butter in a heavy pan, stir in the flour and cook over a low heat to a thick paste. Gradually add the milk, whisking constantly until the sauce boils and thickens, then cook for 1–2 minutes more. Stir in the egg yolks, two-thirds of the Parmesan cheese, the parsley and half the dill. Add salt and ground black pepper to taste.

2 Prepare a 33 x 28cm/13 x 11in Swiss roll tin (jelly roll pan) and preheat the oven to 180°C/350°F/Gas 4. Whisk the egg whites until stiff and fold into the yolk mixture. Pour the mixture into the tin or pan and bake in the oven for 12–15 minutes. Cover with baking parchment and set aside for 10–15 minutes to cool slightly, then tip out on to another sheet of parchment, this time sprinkled with a little Parmesan. Leave to cool.

WHOLE BAKED SALMON

A WHOLE SALMON MAKES A WONDERFUL CENTREPIECE AT PARTIES. TRADITIONALLY IT IS SERVED WITH LEMON AND DILL AND ACCOMPANIED BY VARIOUS SALADS AND A BOWL OF CREAMY MAYONNAISE.

SERVES 10 AS PART OF A BUFFET

INGREDIENTS
  2.25–2.75kg/5–6lb fresh whole
    salmon, cleaned and scaled
  30ml/2 tbsp oil
  1 lemon
  salt and ground black pepper
  lemon wedges, pared cucumber
    ribbons and fresh dill sprigs,
    to garnish

1 Preheat the oven to 150°C/300°F/ Gas 2. Note the weight of the salmon then wash it and dry it well, inside and out. Pour half the oil on to a large piece of strong foil and place the fish in the centre.

2 Put a few slices of lemon inside the salmon and arrange some more on the top. Season well and sprinkle over the remaining oil. Wrap up the foil to make a loose parcel.

COOK'S TIPS
• Use wild, line-caught salmon if you can afford it, preferably from Alaska where fish stocks are healthiest, or buy from a farm where the salmon are humanely treated.
• Use extra wide, extra long foil – sometimes described as turkey foil – to wrap the salmon. This will allow the parcel to be large enough to hold the entire fish comfortably.
• To make the garnish of cucumber ribbons, square off but do not peel a cucumber, then draw a potato peeler down its length.

3 Put the parcel on another sheet of foil or a baking sheet and transfer to the oven. Bake for 8 minutes per 450g/1lb. Check the fish towards the end of cooking and remove from the oven when the flesh is opaque right through. Leave to cool in the foil for 15 minutes.

4 Remove the foil, draining any juices into a jug (pitcher). Use in any recipe requiring fish stock. Peel off the salmon skin. When it is cold, slide the salmon on to a large platter and garnish with lemon wedges, cucumber pared into thin ribbons and sprigs of dill.

SALMON WITH CUCUMBER SAUCE

CUCUMBER AND FRESH DILL ARE A PERFECT COMBINATION IN THIS UNUSUAL HOT SAUCE, WHICH REALLY COMPLEMENTS THE BAKED SALMON.

SERVES 6–8

INGREDIENTS
    1.8kg/4lb salmon, cleaned
      and scaled
    melted butter, for brushing
    3 fresh parsley or thyme sprigs
    ½ lemon, halved
    orange slices and salad leaves,
      to serve

For the cucumber sauce
    1 large cucumber, peeled
    25g/1oz/2 tbsp butter
    120ml/4fl oz/½ cup dry white wine
    45ml/3 tbsp finely chopped
      fresh dill
    60ml/4 tbsp sour cream
    salt and ground black pepper

3 Meanwhile, halve the cucumber lengthways, scoop out the seeds, then dice the flesh.

4 Place the cucumber in a colander, toss lightly with salt and leave for about 30 minutes to drain. Rinse well, drain again and pat dry.

5 Heat the butter in a small pan, add the cucumber and cook for 2 minutes until translucent. Add the wine and boil briskly until the cucumber is dry. Stir in the dill and sour cream and season to taste. Fillet the salmon and serve with the cucumber sauce, orange slices and salad leaves.

1 Season the salmon. Brush it inside and out with melted butter. Place the herb sprigs and lemon in the cavity.

2 Wrap the salmon in foil, folding the edges together securely, then bake in a preheated oven at 220°C/425°F/Gas 7 for 15 minutes. Remove the fish from the oven and leave in the foil for 1 hour, then remove the skin from the salmon.

SALMON AU GRATIN

THIS IS A VERY RICH APPETIZER, PERFECT FOR SERVING BEFORE A RELATIVELY PLAIN MAIN COURSE, SUCH AS A SALAD. THE SALMON IS BAKED IN A LUXURIOUS CREAM AND GRUYÈRE SAUCE.

SERVES 6

INGREDIENTS
  350g/12oz salmon fillet, skinned
    and cubed
  grated rind and juice of 2 limes
  60ml/4 tbsp olive oil
  2 small red onions, sliced
  2 garlic cloves, finely chopped
  bunch of fresh tarragon, chopped
  450ml/¾ pint/scant 2 cups double
    (heavy) cream
  115g/4oz Gruyère cheese,
    grated
  salt and ground black pepper
  country bread, to serve

1 Place the salmon cubes in a bowl and sprinkle the lime rind and juice over. Toss well and leave to stand for 10 minutes. Meanwhile, use 15ml/1 tbsp of the oil to lightly grease six ramekins.

2 Preheat the grill (broiler) to high. Heat the remaining oil in a frying pan over a medium heat, add the onion and fry for 3 minutes. Add the garlic to the pan and cook for a further 3 minutes. Divide the onion mixture among the ramekins.

3 Remove the salmon cubes from the marinade and place them in a clean bowl. Add the tarragon and cream. Season and mix gently.

4 Divide among the ramekins and top with the grated cheese. Support the ramekins on a baking sheet and grill (broil) for 5–6 minutes or until the salmon is cooked and the cheese is golden brown and bubbling. Serve immediately with bread.

VARIATIONS
• Look out for salmon lardons in specialist delicatessens. These, like bacon lardons, are quite chunky, and work well for a recipe like this. They are popular in France, partly because they are full of flavour and partly for convenience, since they are available to buy ready cut.
• Although Gruyère is the preferred cheese for this recipe, Emmental or Jarlsberg could be used instead. Grate the cheese finely – a microplane grater is useful for this.

SALMON FISH CAKES

WHOLEGRAIN MUSTARD GIVES THESE EXCELLENT FISH CAKES A SLIGHT TANG, BARELY DETECTABLE BUT QUITE DELICIOUS. THE FLAVOUR IS ECHOED IN THE MAYONNAISE THAT ACCOMPANIES THEM.

SERVES 4

INGREDIENTS
    450g/1lb cooked salmon fillet
    450g/1lb cooked potatoes, mashed
    25g/1oz/2 tbsp butter, melted
    10ml/2 tsp wholegrain mustard
    15ml/1 tbsp each chopped fresh dill
      and chopped fresh parsley
    grated rind and juice of ½ lemon
    15g/½oz/1 tbsp plain
      (all-purpose) flour
    1 egg, lightly beaten
    150g/5oz/1¼ cups home-made
      dried breadcrumbs
    60ml/4 tbsp sunflower oil
    salt and ground black pepper
    rocket (arugula) leaves and chives,
      to garnish
    lemon wedges, to serve

For the spicy mayonnaise
    350ml/12fl oz/1½ cups mayonnaise
    10ml/2 tsp wholegrain mustard
    2.5–5ml/½–1 tsp Worcestershire sauce
    dash of Tabasco sauce

1 Flake the cooked salmon, discarding any skin and bones. Put it in a bowl with the mashed potato, melted butter and wholegrain mustard, and mix well. Stir in the dill, parsley, lemon rind and juice. Season to taste with salt and pepper.

2 Divide the mixture into eight portions and shape each into a ball, then flatten into a thick disc. Dip the fish cakes first in flour, then in egg and finally in breadcrumbs, making sure that they are evenly coated.

3 Put the salmon fish cakes on a plate and place in the refrigerator to firm up a little. Meanwhile, make the spicy mayonnaise by mixing all the ingredients in a bowl.

4 Heat the oil in a frying pan until it is very hot. Fry the fish cakes in batches until golden brown and crisp all over. As each batch is ready, drain on kitchen paper and keep hot while you fry the rest. Garnish with rocket leaves and chives and serve with the lemon wedges and spicy mayonnaise.

COOK'S TIP
To make the dried breadcrumbs, crumb day-old white bread in a food processor, or grate it into a bowl. Spread out the crumbs on baking sheets and dry in a very low oven. Process again if you like, to produce fine crumbs.

SALMON GOUJONS WITH LIME AND CAPER DIP

THESE SCRUMPTIOUS SALMON STRIPS ARE COATED IN A MIXTURE OF POLENTA AND PAPRIKA BEFORE BEING FRIED. THIS GIVES THEM A REALLY CRISP FINISH WITH A SUBTLE SPICY FLAVOUR.

SERVES 4

INGREDIENTS
    350g/12oz salmon fillet, skinned
    50g/2oz/½ cup plain
       (all-purpose) flour
    2 eggs, beaten
    50g/2oz/⅓ cup polenta
    5ml/1 tsp paprika
    vegetable oil, for deep-frying
    salt and ground black pepper
    lime wedges, to garnish

For the dip
    200ml/7fl oz/scant 1 cup Greek
       (US strained plain) yogurt
    finely grated rind and juice
       of 1 lime
    30ml/2 tbsp drained capers,
       finely chopped

COOK'S TIP
For perfectly crisp goujons ensure that the vegetable oil is very hot before adding the salmon. If the oil is not up to temperature the batter coating the salmon will be soggy.

1 To make the dip, combine all of the ingredients in a bowl and mix. Season and spoon into a serving dish. Cover and chill in the refrigerator.

2 Cut the salmon fillets into strips of 7.5 x 2.5cm/3 x 1in. Season the flour and place in a shallow dish. Pour the beaten egg into a separate shallow dish. Combine the polenta and paprika in a third shallow dish.

3 Dip the salmon strips, one at a time, in the seasoned flour, then in the beaten egg and finally in the polenta, making sure they are evenly coated.

4 Heat the oil for deep-frying until it is very hot. Fry the goujons in batches, about four or five at a time, for 3–5 minutes, turning them occasionally with a slotted spoon.

5 Remove the cooked goujons with a slotted spoon and drain well on a double thickness of kitchen paper. Keep the cooked goujons hot in the oven while you cook the remainder.

6 When all the goujons have been cooked, arrange them on a platter. Garnish them with the lime wedges and serve them with the lime and caper dip.

SMOKED SALMON AND SPINACH WRAPS

THE CREAMY TEXTURES OF AVOCADO AND HUMMUS AND THE VIBRANT COLOURS OF RED PEPPER AND BABY SPINACH MAKE THESE DELICIOUS WRAPS A FEAST FOR THE EYES AS WELL AS THE TASTE BUDS!

MAKES 6

INGREDIENTS
2 red (bell) peppers
30ml/2 tbsp olive oil
6 large wheat flour tortillas
1 avocado
30ml/2 tbsp lemon juice
115g/4oz/½ cup hummus
25g/1oz/3 tbsp pine nuts
50g/2oz baby spinach leaves
115g/4oz smoked salmon
salt and ground black pepper

COOK'S TIP
The peppers can also be charred under the grill (broiler) and the tortillas heated in the microwave.

1 Preheat the oven to 180°C/350°F/Gas 4. Place the peppers in a roasting pan. Drizzle the olive oil over and season with plenty of salt and black pepper. Bake for 25–30 minutes.

2 Peel the skin off the cooked peppers and discard the core and seeds. Cut the pepper flesh into strips.

3 Place the tortillas on a sheet of foil and seal tightly. Warm in the oven for 10 minutes.

4 Meanwhile, cut the avocado in half, remove the stone (pit) and peel, then slice lengthways. Sprinkle with the lemon juice to prevent the avocado flesh from turning brown.

5 Remove the tortillas from the oven. Spread a quarter of the hummus over each wrap, using a round-bladed knife or slim spatula, then sprinkle the pine nuts evenly over the hummus, but leaving the borders free of nuts.

6 Divide the spinach, salmon and peppers among the topped tortillas, placing them in a line down the centre. Roll up each wrap and serve immediately, while still warm. Offer lemon wedges for squeezing, if you like.

POTATO BLINIS WITH SMOKED SALMON

THESE CRISP, LIGHT PANCAKES ORIGINATED IN RUSSIA, WHERE THEY ARE SERVED WITH THE FINEST CAVIAR, BUT THEY ARE ALSO GOOD WITH SALMON ROE.

SERVES 6 AS PART OF A BUFFET

INGREDIENTS
   1 potato, about 115g/4oz, boiled
      and mashed
   15ml/1 tbsp easy-blend (rapid-rise)
      dried yeast
   175g/6oz/1½ cups plain
      (all-purpose) flour
   300ml/½ pint/1¼ cups
      lukewarm water
   oil, for greasing
   90ml/6 tbsp sour cream
   6 slices smoked salmon
   salt and ground black pepper
   lemon slices, to garnish

COOK'S TIP
Leaving the batter to rest will result in lighter, airier blinis.

1 Mix the potato, yeast, flour, salt and pepper with the water to make a smooth dough. Cover with clear film (plastic wrap) and leave to rise in a warm place for 30 minutes until doubled in bulk.

2 Heat a non-stick frying pan and add a little oil. Drop spoonfuls of the mixture on to the pan.

3 Cook the blinis for 2 minutes until lightly golden on the underside. Toss with a spatula and cook on the second side. Remove each batch as it cooks and keep warm.

4 To serve, top each warm blini with a little of the sour cream and a small folded slice of smoked salmon. Garnish the blinis with a grind of black pepper and a small slice of lemon.

VARIATION
For an alternative topping, try mixing 200g/7oz/scant 1 cup cream cheese with 15ml/1 tbsp of chopped parsley or dill. Spread on the blinis and top with the smoked salmon. Add slivers of sweet pickled cherry chillies or a spoonful of delicate pink salmon roe.

SALMON TRIANGLES

THESE ELEGANT PARTY PIECES TAKE A LITTLE TIME TO MAKE, BUT THEY CAN BE PREPARED IN ADVANCE WITH THE FINAL TOUCHES ADDED JUST BEFORE YOUR GUESTS ARRIVE.

MAKES 12

INGREDIENTS
  2 eggs
  3–4 slices dark rye bread
  115g/4oz poached salmon
  coriander (cilantro) leaves, to garnish

For the lime and coriander mayonnaise
  45–60ml/3–4 tbsp mayonnaise
  5ml/1 tsp chopped fresh coriander
    (cilantro)
  5ml/1 tsp freshly squeezed
    lime juice
  salt and ground black pepper

1 Bring a pan of water to the boil. Reduce the heat, then add the eggs. Cook for 12 minutes, then plunge the eggs into cold water to arrest further cooking. When cold, shell the hard-boiled eggs and slice them.

2 Cut the rye bread into 12 triangular pieces, using a sharp knife.

3 Make the lime and coriander mayonnaise. Combine the mayonnaise, chopped coriander and lime juice, and season to taste.

4 Top each bread triangle with a slice of egg, a small portion of salmon and a teaspoon of mayonnaise. Garnish with a coriander leaf. Chill until ready to serve.

VARIATIONS
• Try substituting cherry tomato slices for the egg and topping the salmon with a mixture of mayonnaise and red pesto, or use sliced cucumber and top the salmon with lemon-flavoured mayonnaise.
• For a spicy note, try substituting the coriander for paprika in the mayonnaise and garnish the triangles sparingly with chilli flakes.
• For a luxury note, use a neutral mayonnaise and add a spoonful of caviar. The black roe looks very dramatic with the pale pink salmon.

CEVICHE

THIS IS A FRUITY FIRST COURSE OF MARINATED FRESH FISH. TAKE CARE IN CHOOSING THE FISH FOR THIS DISH; IT MUST BE AS FRESH AS POSSIBLE AND SERVED ON THE DAY IT IS MADE, SINCE IT IS "COOKED" BY THE ACTION OF THE CITRUS JUICES, RATHER THAN A MORE CONVENTIONAL METHOD.

SERVES 6

INGREDIENTS
    350g/12oz medium cooked
      prawns (shrimp)
    350g/12oz scallops, removed from
      their shells, with corals intact
    175g/6oz tomatoes
    1 mango, about 175g/6oz
    1 red onion, finely chopped
    350g/12oz salmon fillet
    1 fresh red chilli, seeded and chopped
    12 limes
    30ml/2 tbsp caster (superfine) sugar
    2 pink grapefruit
    3 oranges
    salt and ground black pepper

1 Set aside two prawns for the garnish. Peel the remaining prawns and cut the scallops into 1.2cm/½in dice.

2 Dice the tomatoes and place in a bowl. Peel the mango, dice the flesh and add it to the bowl with the red onion. Mix well.

3 Skin the salmon, then remove any pin bones with a pair of tweezers. Cut the fish into small pieces and mix with the tomato, mango and onion. Add the chilli and mix well.

4 Squeeze the juice from eight of the limes and add it to the tomato mixture, with the sugar and a little salt and pepper. Stir, cover and leave to marinate in a cool place for 3 hours.

5 Segment the grapefruit, oranges and remaining limes. Drain off as much excess lime juice as possible and mix the fruit segments into the marinated ingredients. Season to taste and serve, garnished with the reserved prawns.

COOK'S TIP
Skinning the salmon fillet will be much easier if you place the fish in the freezer for about 10 minutes first. Cut down to the skin at the narrow end of the fillet, then, holding that end firmly with your free hand, turn the blade and slice the flesh off the skin.

SALMON CEVICHE <u>WITH</u> GIN <u>AND</u> LIME

THE UNUSUAL COMBINATION OF LIME JUICE AND GIN IS NOT ONLY A WONDERFUL MARINADE BUT THE COMBINATION ALSO SERVES TO EFFECTIVELY "COOK" THE RAW SALMON. THE COMBINATION OF PEPPERY CITRUS FLAVOURS IN THIS DISH IS TRULY DELICIOUS.

SERVES 4 AS PART OF A BUFFET

INGREDIENTS

675g/1½lb salmon fillet, skinned
1 small red onion, thinly sliced
6 chives
6 fennel sprigs
3 fresh parsley sprigs
2 limes
30ml/2 tbsp gin
45ml/3 tbsp olive oil
sea salt and ground black pepper
salad leaves, to serve

1 Cut the salmon fillet into thin slices, removing any remaining bones with tweezers. Lay the pieces in a wide, shallow non-metallic dish.

2 Sprinkle over the onion slices and strew with the chives, fennel and parsley sprigs. Using a canelle knife, remove a few fine strips of rind from the limes and reserve for the garnish. Cut off the remaining rind, avoiding the pith, and slice it roughly.

COOK'S TIP

• When preparing salmon in this way, it is vital to use very fresh fish from a reputable source. Tell the fishmonger you intend making ceviche, explaining that the fish will not be cooked in the conventional way, but that the texture will be altered by marinating it in lime juice, gin and olive oil.
• Serve the ceviche on the day you prepare it. It needs to be chilled for 4 hours, but do not leave it for much longer before serving.

3 Squeeze the lime juice into a jug (pitcher). Add the roughly sliced rind, with the gin and olive oil. Stir in sea salt and black pepper to taste. Pour the mixture over the fish and stir gently to coat each piece thoroughly.

4 Cover the dish and refrigerate for 4 hours, stirring occasionally. To serve, arrange the slices of marinated fish on a platter, with the salad leaves. Sprinkle over the reserved strips of lime rind as a garnish.

VARIATIONS

• For an oriental flavour, try substituting the gin for sake, mirin or a dry sherry and garnishing with coriander, basil and chopped chillies as an alternative to the chives, fennel and parsley.
• Citrus juices are an essential element for a ceviche to work properly. This recipe uses lime juice, but lemons, oranges and grapefruit make good alternatives.

GRAVLAX

BE GENEROUS WITH THE DILL IN THIS SCANDINAVIAN SPECIALITY — IT ADDS A LOVELY FLAVOUR.

<u>SERVES 12</u>

INGREDIENTS
    1.2kg/2½lb salmon, cleaned and
      with head, tail and bones removed
    45ml/3 tbsp coarse sea salt
    30ml/2 tbsp caster
      (superfine) sugar
    12 black peppercorns, crushed
    large bunch of fresh dill, chopped

For the mustard sauce
    2 egg yolks
    30ml/2 tbsp white wine vinegar
    45ml/3 tbsp mild mustard
    50g/2oz soft light brown sugar
    300ml/½ pint/1¼ cups light olive oil
    30ml/2 tbsp chopped fresh dill
    salt and ground white pepper

1 Place one fillet skin-side down in a non-metallic dish. Sprinkle over the salt, sugar and peppercorns. Cover with half the dill.

2 Lay the other fillet on top and cover with the remaining dill. Set a heavy weight on top of the fish. Cover and chill in the refrigerator for at least 72 hours, turning the salmon every 12 hours and basting it with the brine solution that collects in the dish.

3 Put the egg yolks and half the vinegar and mustard into a food processor. Add the brown sugar and a little salt and white pepper. Process until smooth.

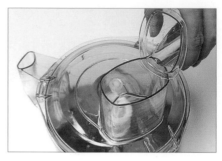

4 With the motor running, gradually add the oil in a steady stream through the feeder tube, continuing to process the mixture until it thickens. Stir in the remaining vinegar and mustard with the dill, then scrape the sauce into a bowl and set it aside.

5 Drain the liquid from the salmon and scrape off any remaining salt. Pat the fish dry. Cut on the diagonal into thin slices and serve with the mustard sauce.

CHILLI AND SALT-CURED SALMON

BUY VERY FRESH FISH FROM A REPUTABLE SOURCE FOR THIS DELICIOUS ALTERNATIVE TO SMOKED SALMON.

SERVES 10

INGREDIENTS
  50g/2oz/¼ cup sea salt
  45ml/3 tbsp caster
    (superfine) sugar
  5ml/1 tsp chilli powder
  5ml/1 tsp ground black pepper
  45ml/3 tbsp chopped fresh
    coriander (cilantro)
  2 salmon fillets, about
    250g/9oz each
  fresh flat leaf parsley, to garnish
  garlic mayonnaise, to serve

VARIATIONS
• Sweet chilli dipping sauce makes an excellent alternative to the garlic mayonnaise used in this recipe.
• The salt is an essential component in cooking the salmon, but beyond this you can adapt the spice rub to suit your individual tastes.

1 In a bowl, mix together the salt, sugar, chilli powder, pepper and coriander. Rub the mixture into the salmon flesh.

2 Place one of the fillets, skin side down, in a shallow glass dish. Place the other fillet on top, with the skin side up. Cover with foil, then place a weight on top.

3 Chill for 48 hours, turning the fish every 8 hours or so and basting it with the liquid that forms in the dish.

4 Drain the salmon well and transfer to a board. Using a sharp knife, slice it diagonally into wafer-thin slices. Arrange on plates and garnish with sprigs of parsley. Serve with garlic mayonnaise.

COOK'S TIP
For a garnish for the salt-cured salmon, scrape any remaining fish off the skin. Cut the skin into 1cm/½in wide strips and fry for 1 minute in hot oil until crisp. Drain and cool on kitchen paper.

SALMON MARINATED WITH THAI SPICES

MARINATING THE FISH IN AN AROMATIC MIXTURE OF GINGER, LEMON GRASS, LIME LEAVES, CHILLIES AND SALT NOT ONLY CURES IT, BUT ALSO IMBUES THE SALMON WITH DELECTABLE FLAVOURS.

SERVES 4–6 AS PART OF A BUFFET

INGREDIENTS

   tail piece of 1 salmon, about
      675g/1½lb, halved and boned
      to produce two fillets
   20ml/4 tsp coarse sea salt
   20ml/4 tsp sugar
   2.5cm/1in piece fresh root
      ginger, grated
   2 lemon grass stalks, coarse outer
      leaves removed, thinly sliced
   4 kaffir lime leaves, finely chopped
      or shredded
   grated rind of 1 lime
   1 fresh red chilli, seeded and
      finely chopped
   5ml/1 tsp black peppercorns,
      coarsely crushed
   30ml/2 tbsp chopped fresh
      coriander (cilantro)
   fresh coriander (cilantro) and kaffir
      limes, to garnish

For the dressing
   150ml/¼ pint/⅔ cup mayonnaise
   juice of ½ lime
   10ml/2 tsp chopped fresh
      coriander (cilantro)

1 Make the dressing by mixing the mayonnaise, lime juice and chopped coriander in a bowl. Place in the refrigerator until needed.

2 Remove any remaining bones from the salmon, using a pair of tweezers. In a bowl, mix together the salt, sugar, ginger, lemon grass, lime leaves, lime rind, chilli, peppercorns and chopped fresh coriander.

3 Place one-quarter of the spice mixture in a shallow non-metallic dish. Place one salmon fillet, skin side down, on top of the spices. Spread two-thirds of the remaining mixture over the flesh then place the remaining fillet on top, flesh side down. Sprinkle the rest of the spice mixture over the fish.

4 Cover the fish with foil, then place a board on top. Add some weights, such as clean cans of fruit. Chill for 4–5 days, turning the fish daily.

5 Scrape the spices off the fish and slice it thinly. Garnish with coriander and lime wedges and serve with the dressing.

MOOLI LAYERED WITH SMOKED SALMON

THIS TRADITIONAL JAPANESE RECIPE ORIGINALLY CALLED FOR SALTED SLICED SALMON AND MOOLI TO BE PICKLED IN A WOODEN BARREL FOR A LONG TIME. THIS VERSION IS LESS SALTY AND FAR QUICKER.

SERVES 4

INGREDIENTS

10cm/4in mooli (daikon), about
  6cm/2½in in diameter, peeled
10ml/2 tsp salt
5ml/1 tsp rice vinegar
5cm/2in square dashi-konbu (dried
  kelp seaweed), chopped into
  1cm/½in strips
50g/2oz smoked salmon, thinly sliced
2.5ml/½ tsp white poppy seeds

1 Slice the mooli very thinly into rounds. Put in a shallow container, sprinkle with salt and vinegar, and add the chopped dashi-konbu. Mix and rub gently with your hands. Cover and leave in the refrigerator for 1 hour.

2 Drain in a sieve and squeeze out the excess liquid. If necessary, rinse with running water for 30 seconds, then drain and squeeze out again.

3 Cut the smoked salmon slices into 4cm/1½in squares. Take one slice of mooli, top with a salmon slice, then cover with another mooli slice. Repeat this process until all the salmon is used.

4 Place the tower of salmon and mooli in a shallow container, cover with clear film (plastic wrap), then leave to pickle at room temperature for up to 1 day.

5 Arrange the mooli rounds on a serving plate and put a pinch of poppy seeds in the centre.

COOK'S TIPS
• Use a good quality salmon for this recipe as the flavour of cheaper varieties is often obscured by the smoking process.
• You can use a mandoline, a food cutter or a vegetable slicer to make paper-thin slices of mooli.

HAND-MOULDED SUSHI

IF YOU HAVE ACCESS TO QUALITY SEAFOOD AT THE PEAK OF FRESHNESS, THIS IS A WONDERFUL WAY OF APPRECIATING ITS SUPERB NATURAL FLAVOUR.

SERVES 4

INGREDIENTS

400g/14oz/2 cups Japanese short
  grain rice, soaked for 20 minutes
  in water to cover
500ml/18fl oz/2½ cups water
55ml/3½ tbsp rice vinegar, plus
  extra for moulding
30ml/2 tbsp caster (superfine) sugar
10ml/2 tsp salt
4 raw king prawns (jumbo shrimp),
  head and shell removed, tails intact
4 scallops, white muscle only
425g/15oz assorted very fresh fish,
  such as salmon, tuna and sea bass,
  skinned, cleaned and filleted
45ml/3 tbsp wasabi paste
pickled ginger, to garnish
shoyu (Japanese soy sauce), to serve

1 Drain the rice, then put it in a pan with the measured water. Bring to the boil, then reduce the heat, cover and simmer for 20 minutes, until the water has been absorbed. Meanwhile, heat the vinegar, sugar and salt in a pan, stir well and cool. Fold into the rice, then remove the pan from the heat, cover and leave to stand for 20 minutes.

2 Insert a bamboo skewer into each prawn lengthways. This stops the prawns curling up when cooked. Boil them in lightly salted water for 2 minutes, or until they turn pink. Drain and cool, then pull out the skewers. Cut open from the belly side but do not slice in two. With the point of a sharp knife, remove the black vein running down the back. Open each prawn out flat and place on a tray.

3 Slice the scallops horizontally in half, but not quite through. Gently open each scallop at this "hinge" to make a butterfly shape. Place on the tray, cut side down. Use a sharp knife to cut all the fillets into 7.5 x 4cm/3 x 1½in pieces, 5mm/¼in thick. Place all the fish on the tray, cover with clear film (plastic wrap), then chill for at least 1 hour, or up to 4 hours.

4 Spoon the vinegared rice into a bowl. Have ready a small bowl filled with water acidulated with rice vinegar for moulding. Take the tray of seafood from the refrigerator.

5 Wet your hand with the vinegared water and scoop about 25ml/1½ tbsp vinegared rice into your palm. Gently but firmly grip it to make a rectangular block. Do not squash the rice, but ensure that the grains stick together. The size of the blocks must be smaller than the toppings.

6 Put the rice block on a damp chopping board. Taking a piece of fish in your palm, rub a little wasabi paste in the middle of it. Put the rice block on top of the fish and gently press it. Form your palm into a cup and shape the topped rice to a smooth-surfaced mound.

7 Repeat this process until all of the rice and toppings are used. Serve at once with a little shoyu dribbled on each plate. To eat, pick up a piece of sushi and dip into the shoyu. Refresh your mouth with pickled ginger between pieces.

SALMON <u>AND</u> RICE TRIANGLES

IN JAPAN, WHERE THESE ORIGINATED, THEY ARE OFTEN USED FOR PACKED LUNCHES OR PICNICS, BUT WOULD ALSO MAKE ELEGANT PARTY PIECES. THEY ARE GREAT FUN TO MAKE AND LOOK MARVELLOUS.

<u>SERVES 4 AS PART OF A BUFFET</u>

INGREDIENTS
   1 salmon steak
   15ml/1 tbsp salt
   450g/1lb/4 cups freshly cooked
      Japanese short grain rice
   4 umeboshi (plum pickles)
   ½ sheet yaki-nori seaweed, cut into
      four equal strips
   white and black sesame seeds,
      for sprinkling

1 Grill (broil) the salmon steak for 4–5 minutes on each side, until the flesh flakes easily when it is tested with the tip of a sharp knife. Set aside to cool. When the salmon is cold, flake it, discarding any skin and bones.

2 Put the salt in a bowl. Spoon a quarter of the warm cooked rice into a small rice bowl. Make a hole in the middle of the rice and put in one umeboshi. Smooth the rice carefully over to cover it completely.

3 Wet the palms of both hands with cold water, then rub the salt evenly on to your palms. Empty the rice and umeboshi from the bowl on to one hand. Use both hands to shape the rice into a triangular shape, using firm but not heavy pressure. Make three more rice triangles in the same way.

4 Mix the flaked salmon into the remaining rice, then shape it into triangles as before.

5 Wrap a strip of yaki-nori around each of the umeboshi triangles. Sprinkle sesame seeds on the salmon triangles.

COOK'S TIP
Always use warm rice to make triangles. Allow them to cool completely and wrap each in foil or plastic wrap.

COMPRESSED SUSHI <u>WITH</u> SMOKED SALMON

THIS SIMPLE RECIPE OF VINEGARED RICE WITH SMOKED SALMON IS AN EXCELLENT INTRODUCTION TO THE ANCIENT ART OF SUSHI AND IS IDEAL FOR ANYONE NERVOUS ABOUT EATING RAW FISH.

MAKES ABOUT 12

INGREDIENTS
200g/7oz/1 cup Japanese short grain rice, soaked for 20 minutes in water to cover
250ml/8fl oz/1 cup water
40ml/8 tsp rice vinegar, plus extra for moulding
20ml/4 tsp caster (superfine) sugar
5ml/1 tsp salt
175g/6oz smoked salmon, thickly sliced
15ml/1 tbsp sake
15ml/1 tbsp water
30ml/2 tbsp shoyu (Japanese soy sauce)
1 lemon, thinly sliced into 6 x 3mm/1/8in rings

1 Drain the rice, then put it in a pan with the measured water. Bring to the boil, then reduce the heat, cover and simmer for 20 minutes, until all the water has been absorbed. Meanwhile, heat the vinegar, sugar and salt in a pan, stir well and cool. Fold into the hot rice, then remove from the heat, cover and leave to stand for 20 minutes.

2 Lay the smoked salmon on a chopping board and sprinkle with a mixture of the sake, water and shoyu. Leave to marinate for 1 hour, then wipe dry with kitchen paper.

3 Wet a wooden Japanese sushi mould or line a 25 x 7.5 x 5cm/10 x 3 x 2in plastic container with a large sheet of clear film (plastic wrap), allowing the edges to hang over.

4 Spread half the smoked salmon to evenly cover the bottom of the mould or container. Add one-quarter of the cooked rice and firmly press down with hands dampened with rice vinegar to make a layer 1cm/1/2in thick. Add the remainder of the salmon, and press the remaining rice on top.

5 Put the wet wooden lid on the mould, or cover the plastic container with the overhanging clear film. Place a weight, such as a heavy dinner plate, on top. Leave in a cool place overnight, or for at least 3 hours. If you use the refrigerator, place the mould in the least cool part, such as on the top shelf.

6 Remove the compressed sushi from the mould or container and unwrap. Cut into 2cm/3/4in slices and serve on a Japanese lacquered tray or a large plate. Quarter the lemon rings. Garnish each piece of sushi with two pieces of lemon and serve.

SIMPLE ROLLED SUSHI

SALMON MAKES A SUPERB FILLING FOR THESE SIMPLE ROLLS. ALSO KNOWN AS HOSO-MAKI, THEY MAKE EXCELLENT CANAPÉS. YOU WILL NEED A BAMBOO MAT FOR THE ROLLING PROCESS.

MAKES 12 ROLLS OR 72 SLICES

INGREDIENTS
400g/14oz/2 cups Japanese short
  grain rice, soaked for 20 minutes
  in water to cover
550ml/18fl oz/2¼ cups cold water
55ml/3½ tbsp rice vinegar
15ml/1 tbsp sugar
10ml/2 tsp salt
6 sheets yaki-nori
200g/7oz very fresh salmon fillet
200g/7oz very fresh tuna, in
  one piece
wasabi paste
½ cucumber, quartered lengthways
  and seeded
salmon roe and pickled ginger,
  to garnish (optional)
shoyu (Japanese soy sauce), to serve

1 Drain the rice, then put it in a pan with the measured water. Bring to the boil, then lower the heat, cover and simmer for 20 minutes, or until all the liquid has been absorbed. Meanwhile, heat the vinegar, sugar and salt in a pan, stir well and cool. Fold into the hot rice, then remove the pan from the heat, cover and leave to stand for 20 minutes.

2 Cut the yaki-nori sheets in half. Cut the salmon and tuna into sticks the length of the long side of the yaki-nori and 1cm/½in square if viewed end-on.

3 Place a sheet of yaki-nori, shiny side down, on a bamboo mat. Divide the rice into 12 portions. Spread one portion over the yaki-nori, leaving a 1cm/½in clear space around the edges.

4 Spread a little wasabi paste in a horizontal line along the middle of the rice and lay one or two sticks of tuna lengthways on this, so that when rolled, the tuna will form a filling.

5 Holding the mat and the edge of the yaki-nori nearest to you, roll up the yaki-nori and rice into a cylinder with the tuna in the middle. Use the mat as a guide – do not roll it into the food. Roll the rice tightly so that it sticks together.

6 Carefully roll the sushi off the mat. Make 11 more rolls in the same way, four for each filling ingredient, but do not use wasabi with the cucumber. Use a wet knife to cut each roll into six slices and stand them on a platter. Garnish the sushi with salmon roe and pickled ginger, if you wish, and serve with shoyu.

LIGHT LUNCHES AND SIMPLE SUPPERS

Salmon cooks extremely quickly, so is ideal for occasions when you want good food fast. The recipes in this chapter are all light and simple to prepare, yet still delicious, whether you fancy a sophisticated brunch of Scrambled Eggs with Smoked Salmon, a decadent lunch of Creamy Lemon and Salmon Pappardelle or a healthy supper such as Salmon Kebabs with Coconut. Also on the menu are old favourites like Salmon Quiche with Potato Pastry and Lox with Bagels and Cream Cheese.

LOX WITH BAGELS AND CREAM CHEESE

THIS GLORIOUSLY COMFORTING DISH IS PERFECT FOR A WEEKEND BREAKFAST OR A LIGHT LUNCH WITH FRIENDS. THIS RECIPE IS A JEWISH DELI CLASSIC WHICH YOU CAN EASILY RECREATE AT HOME.

SERVES 2

INGREDIENTS
2 bagels
115–175g/4–6oz/½–¾ cup full-fat
  cream cheese
150g/5oz sliced best
  smoked salmon
ground black pepper
lemon wedges, to serve

1 Preheat the oven to 200ºC/400ºF/ Gas 6. Put the bagels on a large baking sheet and warm them in the oven for 4–5 minutes.

2 Remove the bagels from the oven, split them in two and spread generously with cream cheese. Pile the salmon on top of the bagels and grind over plenty of black pepper.

3 Squeeze over some lemon juice, then top with the other bagel half and eat while still warm.

4 For an easy and elegant touch, place a wedge of lemon in the centre of a small square of muslin (cheesecloth), bring up the edges to enclose it, tie with fine string and put it on the plate. This will ensure that no pips find their way into the food.

COOK'S TIP
It is essential to be generous with the smoked salmon and to use the best cream cheese you can find – although healthier, low-fat versions are available, the best flavour comes from decadent, full-fat cream cheese.

SALMON QUICHE <u>WITH</u> POTATO PASTRY

THERE ARE SO MANY WONDERFUL WAYS OF USING SMOKED SALMON. HERE IT FORMS THE FILLING FOR A LIGHT BUT RICHLY-FLAVOURED QUICHE MADE WITH MELT-IN-THE-MOUTH POTATO PASTRY.

SERVES 6

INGREDIENTS
115g/4oz floury potatoes, diced
225g/8oz/2 cups plain (all-purpose) flour, sifted
115g/4oz/½ cup butter, diced
½ egg, beaten
10ml/2 tsp chilled water
salad leaves and chopped fresh dill, to serve

For the filling
6 eggs, beaten
150ml/¼ pint/⅔ cup full cream (whole) milk
300ml/½ pint/1¼ cups double (heavy) cream
30–45ml/2–3 tbsp chopped fresh dill
30ml/2 tbsp drained bottled capers, chopped
275g/10oz smoked salmon
salt and ground black pepper

1 Cook the potatoes in a large pan of salted boiling water for 15 minutes or until tender. Drain through a colander and return to the pan. Mash the potatoes until smooth and set aside to cool.

2 Place the flour in a bowl and rub in the butter to form fine crumbs. Beat in the potatoes and egg. Bring the mixture together, adding chilled water if needed.

3 Roll the pastry out on a floured surface to a 28cm/11in round. Loop the pastry over the rolling pin and ease it into a deep, 23cm/9in round, loose-based, fluted flan tin (pan). Trim the edges. Chill for 1 hour.

4 Preheat the oven to 200°C/400°F/ Gas 6. Place a flat baking sheet in the oven to heat it. Using a sharp cook's knife or a pair of kitchen scissors, chop the smoked salmon into small bitesize pieces. Place the smoked salmon on a plate, cover, and set it aside for later.

5 Now make the filling. In a large mixing bowl, beat the eggs with the milk and double cream. Stir in the fresh chopped dill and the bottled capers and season generously with black pepper. Add in the chopped salmon and stir with a wooden spoon or spatula to combine thoroughly.

6 Remove the pastry case (pie shell) from the refrigerator, prick the base well and pour the mixture into it. Bake on a baking sheet for 35–45 minutes. Serve warm with mixed salad leaves and some more dill.

SCRAMBLED EGGS WITH SMOKED SALMON

FOR A LUXURY BREAKFAST, OR A LATE-NIGHT SUPPER, YOU CAN'T BEAT THIS SPECIAL COMBINATION. SERVE IT WITH BUCK'S FIZZ: CHAMPAGNE MIXED WITH FRESHLY SQUEEZED ORANGE JUICE.

SERVES 4

INGREDIENTS
    4 slices of pumpernickel or
      wholemeal (whole-wheat) bread,
      crusts trimmed
    50g/2oz/¼ cup butter
    115g/4oz thinly sliced
      smoked salmon
    6 eggs
    105ml/7 tbsp crème fraîche or
      sour cream
    salt and ground black pepper
    generous 60ml/4 tbsp salmon roe
      or lumpfish roe and sprigs of dill,
      to garnish

VARIATION
If you are feeling decadent and are lucky enough to have a truffle, another treat is to grate a little into the scrambled eggs. Serve them on toast, topped with a little chopped fresh chervil.

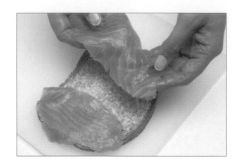

1 Spread the slices of pumpernickel or wholemeal bread with half of the butter and arrange the smoked salmon on top. Cut each slice in half, place two halves on each serving plate and set aside while you make the scrambled eggs.

2 Lightly beat the eggs in a bowl and season with salt and freshly ground pepper. Melt the remaining butter in a pan until sizzling, then quickly stir in the beaten eggs.

3 Stir constantly until the eggs begin to thicken. Just before they have finished cooking, remove the saucepan from the heat and stir in the crème fraîche or sour cream. Set the eggs aside and keep warm.

4 Spoon the scrambled eggs on to the smoked salmon. Top each serving with a spoonful of salmon roe or lumpfish roe and serve, garnished with sprigs of dill.

CZECH-STYLE BAKED SALMON

THIS CENTRAL EUROPEAN WAY OF COOKING SALMON IS VERY EASY, AND THE RESULTS ARE EXCELLENT. THE FISH COOKS IN ITS OWN JUICES, WITH CARAWAY SEEDS ADDING THEIR OWN INIMITABLE FLAVOUR.

SERVES 6

INGREDIENTS

1.8kg/4lb whole salmon, cleaned
115g/4oz/½ cup butter, melted
2.5–5ml/½–1 tsp
  caraway seeds
45ml/3 tbsp lemon juice
salt and ground black pepper
sprigs of flat leaf parsley and lemon
  wedges, to garnish

COOK'S TIP
Take care when slicing off the fins from the salmon as the bones in the fish can be sharp enough to cut fingers, wearing rubber gloves can help prevent this.

1 Preheat the oven to 180°C/350°F/ Gas 4. Scale the salmon, carefully remove the head and tail and slice off the fins with a sharp filleting knife, then cut the fish in half lengthways.

2 Place the prepared salmon, skin side down, in a lightly greased roasting pan. Brush both fillets with the melted butter. Season generously with salt and ground black pepper, sprinkle over the caraway seeds and drizzle with lemon juice.

3 Cover the salmon loosely with foil and bake for 25 minutes. Remove it from the oven, lift off the foil and test the fish. It is done if it is opaque and flakes easily when tested with the point of a knife. Bake for a little longer if needed.

4 Remove the foil and carefully lift the fish on to a serving plate, using two fish slices or large spatulas. Garnish with flat leaf parsley and lemon wedges. The baked salmon can be served straight away, but also tastes good cold.

GRILLED BUTTERFLIED SALMON

DISTINCTIVE JUNIPER BERRIES AND FIERY PEPPERCORNS MELD BEAUTIFULLY WITH THE DELICIOUSLY CLEAN FLAVOUR OF SIMPLE GRILLED SALMON IN THIS HEALTHY AND TEMPTING DISH.

SERVES 6–8

INGREDIENTS
 25ml/1½ tbsp dried
  juniper berries
 10ml/2 tsp dried
  green peppercorns
 5ml/1 tsp caster
  (superfine) sugar
 45ml/3 tbsp vegetable oil, plus extra
  for greasing
 30ml/2 tbsp lemon juice
 2.25kg/5–5¼lb salmon, scaled,
  cleaned and boned for butterflying
salt
 lemon wedges and fresh parsley
  sprigs, to garnish

1 Coarsely grind the juniper berries and peppercorns in a spice mill or in a mortar with a pestle. Put the ground spices in a small bowl and stir in the caster sugar, vegetable oil, lemon juice and salt to taste.

2 Open the salmon like a book, skin side down. Spread the juniper mixture evenly over the flesh. Fold the salmon closed again and place it on a large plate. Cover and marinate in the refrigerator for at least 1 hour.

3 Preheat the grill (broiler). Open up the salmon again and place it, skin side down, on a large oiled baking sheet. Spoon any juniper mixture left on the plate over the top of the fish.

4 Grill (broil) the salmon, keeping it about 10cm/4in from the heat, for 8–10 minutes or until the salmon is cooked and the flesh is opaque. Serve immediately, garnished with the lemon wedges and parsley.

COOK'S TIPS
• Ask your fishmonger to bone the salmon for butterflying. If you order the fish in advance, and give the supplier plenty of time, most will be happy to oblige.
• It is worth keeping a jar of juniper berries in the spice rack, not merely so you can try this recipe, but also for using with game, or to give chicken or rabbit a gamey flavour.

SALMON WITH LEEKS AND PEPPERS

COOKING SALMON IN PAPER PARCELS IS A HEALTHY OPTION. THE FISH AND VEGETABLES COOK IN THEIR OWN JUICES, SO BOTH RETAIN ALL THEIR VALUABLE NUTRIENTS.

SERVES 6

INGREDIENTS

25ml/1½ tbsp groundnut (peanut) oil
2 yellow (bell) peppers, seeded and thinly sliced
4cm/1½in fresh root ginger, peeled and finely shredded
1 large fennel bulb, thinly sliced, fronds chopped and reserved
1 fresh green chilli, seeded and finely shredded
2 large leeks, cut into 10cm/4in lengths and shredded lengthways
30ml/2 tbsp chopped fresh chives
10ml/2 tsp light soy sauce
6 portions salmon fillet, each weighing about 150–175g/ 5–6oz, skinned
10ml/2 tsp toasted sesame oil
salt and ground black pepper

1 Heat the oil in a large frying pan. Add the yellow peppers, ginger and fennel bulb and cook, stirring occasionally, for 5–6 minutes, until they are softened, but not browned.

2 Add the chilli and leeks to the pan and cook, stirring occasionally, for about 3 minutes. Stir in half the chopped chives and the soy sauce and season to taste with a little salt and pepper. Set the vegetable mixture aside to cool slightly.

3 Preheat the oven to 190°C/375°F/ Gas 5. Cut six 35cm/14in rounds of baking parchment or foil and set aside.

4 When the vegetable mixture is cool, divide it equally among the paper or foil rounds and top each with a piece of salmon fillet.

5 Drizzle each portion of fish with a little sesame oil and sprinkle with the remaining chives and the chopped fennel fronds. Season with a little more salt and ground black pepper.

6 Fold the baking parchment or foil over to enclose the fish, rolling and twisting the edges together to seal the parcels.

7 Place the parcels on a baking sheet and bake for 15–20 minutes, or until the parcels have puffed up. Carefully transfer the parcels to six warmed plates and serve immediately, to be opened at the table.

PEPPERED SALMON STEAKS

PINK PEPPERCORNS NOT ONLY MATCH THE DELICATE COLOUR OF SALMON, BUT ALSO COMPLEMENT ITS FLAVOUR. THIS IS A LIGHT DISH, WHICH LOOKS VERY PRETTY WITH ITS SMOKED SALMON TOPPING.

2 Sprinkle the dill over the leeks and courgettes and put the salmon steaks in a single layer on top.

3 Place the pink peppercorns in a mortar and crush them lightly with a pestle until about half the corns are broken. Top the salmon with the peppercorns and the bay leaves.

4 Pour the wine over the steaks and dot with the butter. Season well, cover tightly using foil and bake for 20–25 minutes.

SERVES 4

INGREDIENTS

   1 leek, cut into fine strips
   2 courgettes (zucchini), cut into
    fine strips
   15ml/1 tbsp olive oil
   15ml/1 tbsp chopped fresh dill
   4 salmon steaks
   10ml/2 tsp pink peppercorns
   8 small bay leaves
   150ml/¼ pint/⅔ cup dry white wine
   15g/½oz/1 tbsp butter
   50g/2oz smoked salmon
   20ml/4 tsp salmon roe
   salt and ground black pepper

1 Preheat the oven to 190°C/375°F/ Gas 5. Mix the leek and courgette strips with the oil in a bowl. Toss to coat, then spread out on the base of a shallow baking dish.

5 Cut the smoked salmon into strips. Serve each steak on a bed of the braised leek and courgette mixture and top each portion with smoked salmon strips and salmon roe.

SALMON RISOTTO <u>WITH</u> CUCUMBER

THIS SIMPLE RISOTTO IS COOKED ALL IN ONE GO, AND IS THEREFORE EASIER TO MAKE THAN THE USUAL RISOTTO. NEVERTHELESS, IT IS VERY CREAMY AND THE SALMON GIVES IT SUPERB FLAVOUR.

SERVES 4

INGREDIENTS
  25g/1oz/2 tbsp butter
  small bunch of spring onions
    (scallions), white parts only, chopped
  ½ cucumber, peeled, seeded
    and chopped
  350g/12oz/1¾ cups risotto rice
  1.2 litres/2 pints/5 cups hot fish or
    chicken stock
  150ml/¼ pint/⅔ cup dry white wine
  450g/1lb salmon fillet, skinned
    and diced
  45ml/3 tbsp chopped fresh tarragon
  salt and ground black pepper

3 Stir in the diced salmon and then season. Continue cooking for a further 5 minutes, stirring occasionally, then switch off the heat. Cover the pan and leave the risotto to stand for 5 minutes.

4 Remove the lid from the pan, add the chopped tarragon to the rice and mix lightly. Spoon into a warmed bowl and serve. Offer extra chopped tarragon on the side, if you like.

1 Heat the butter and cook the spring onions and cucumber. Cook for 2 minutes without letting the onions brown.

2 Stir in the rice, then pour in the stock and wine. Bring to the boil, then lower the heat and simmer, uncovered, for 10 minutes, stirring occasionally.

VARIATION
Carnaroli rice would be excellent in this risotto, but if it is not available, arborio rice can be used instead.

RICE CAKES WITH SMOKED SALMON

THESE ELEGANT RICE CAKES ARE MADE USING A RISOTTO BASE. YOU COULD SKIP THIS STAGE AND USE LEFTOVER SEAFOOD OR MUSHROOM RISOTTO INSTEAD. A TOMATO RISOTTO WOULD ALSO WORK WELL.

SERVES 4

INGREDIENTS
  30ml/2 tbsp olive oil
  1 medium onion, chopped
  225g/8oz/generous 1 cup risotto rice
  about 90ml/6 tbsp white wine
  about 750ml/1¼ pints/3 cups fish or
    chicken stock
  15g/½oz/2 tbsp dried porcini
    mushrooms, soaked for 10 minutes
    in warm water to cover
  15ml/1 tbsp chopped fresh parsley
  15ml/1 tbsp chopped fresh chives
  5ml/1 tsp chopped fresh dill
  1 egg, lightly beaten
  about 45ml/3 tbsp ground rice, plus
    extra for dusting
  oil, for frying
  60ml/4 tbsp sour cream
  175g/6oz smoked salmon
  salt and ground black pepper
  radicchio and oakleaf salad, tossed in
    French dressing, to serve

1 Heat the olive oil in a pan and fry the onion for 3–4 minutes until soft. Add the rice and cook, stirring, until the grains are thoroughly coated in oil. Pour in the wine and stock, a little at a time, stirring constantly over a gentle heat until each quantity of liquid has been absorbed before adding more.

2 Drain the mushrooms and chop them into small pieces. When the rice is tender, and all the liquid has been absorbed, stir in the mushrooms, parsley, chives and dill, with salt and pepper to taste. Remove from the heat and set aside for a few minutes to cool.

3 Add the beaten egg, then stir in enough ground rice to bind the mixture – it should be soft but manageable. Dust your hands with ground rice and shape the mixture into four patties, each about 13cm/5in in diameter and about 2cm/¾in thick.

4 Heat the oil and fry the rice cakes for 4–5 minutes until browned on both sides. Drain and cool slightly. Place each rice cake on a plate and top with 15ml/1 tbsp sour cream. Twist two or three slices of smoked salmon on top, and serve with a dressed salad garnish.

FARFALLE WITH SMOKED SALMON AND DILL

THIS QUICK, LUXURIOUS SAUCE FOR PASTA IS VERY FASHIONABLE IN ITALY. DILL IS THE CLASSIC HERB FOR COOKING WITH FISH, BUT IF YOU DON'T LIKE ITS ANISEED FLAVOUR, TRY PARSLEY OR TARRAGON.

2 Add the wine or vermouth and boil hard to reduce to about 30ml/2 tbsp. Stir in the cream and add salt, pepper and nutmeg to taste. Bring to the boil, then simmer for 2–3 minutes until slightly thickened.

3 Cut the smoked salmon slices into 2.5cm/1in squares and stir into the sauce, together with the dill. Add a little lemon juice to taste. Keep the sauce warm until needed.

SERVES 4

INGREDIENTS

  6 spring onions (scallions), sliced
  50g/2oz/¼ cup butter
  90ml/6 tbsp dry white wine
    or vermouth
  450ml/¾ pint/scant 2 cups double
    (heavy) cream
  freshly grated nutmeg
  225g/8oz smoked salmon
  30ml/2 tbsp chopped fresh dill
  freshly squeezed lemon juice
  450g/1lb/4 cups farfalle
  salt and ground black pepper
  fresh dill sprigs, to garnish

1 Using a sharp cook's knife, slice the spring onions finely. Melt the butter in a large pan and fry the spring onions for about 1 minute, stirring occasionally, until softened.

4 Cook the pasta in a large pan of boiling salted water, following the instructions on the packet. Drain well. Toss with the sauce. Spoon into serving bowls and serve immediately, garnished with sprigs of dill.

PENNE <u>WITH</u> CREAM <u>AND</u> SMOKED SALMON

NO SUPPER DISH COULD BE SIMPLER. FRESHLY COOKED PASTA IS TOSSED WITH CREAM, SMOKED SALMON AND THYME. FROM START TO FINISH IT TAKES UNDER 15 MINUTES TO MAKE.

SERVES 4

INGREDIENTS
   350g/12oz/3 cups
      dried penne
   115g/4oz thinly sliced
      smoked salmon
   2–3 fresh thyme sprigs
   25g/1oz/2 tbsp butter
   150ml/¼ pint/⅔ cup double
      (heavy) cream
   salt and ground black pepper

VARIATIONS
• Substitute low-fat cream cheese for half the cream in the sauce, for a less rich mixture that still tastes very good.
• For a more substantial, but equally delicious, dish, add some prawns to the dish alongside the smoked salmon.
• Grate some Parmesan into the cream sauce to add an authentic Italian flavour. Use as little, or as much, as you like.

1 Bring a large pan of lightly salted water to the boil. Add the pasta and cook for about 12 minutes, or according to the instructions on the packet, until the penne are tender but still firm to the bite.

2 Meanwhile, using kitchen scissors or a small, sharp knife, cut the smoked salmon into thin strips, each about 5mm/¼in wide, and place on a plate. Strip the leaves from the thyme sprigs.

3 Melt the butter in a large pan. Stir in the cream with a quarter of the salmon and thyme leaves, then season with pepper. Heat gently for 3–4 minutes, stirring constantly. Do not allow the sauce to boil. Taste for seasoning.

4 Drain the pasta, return it to the pan, and toss it in the cream and salmon sauce. Divide among four warmed bowls and top with the remaining salmon and thyme leaves. Serve immediately.

SPAGHETTI WITH SALMON AND PRAWNS

THIS IS A LOVELY, FRESH-TASTING PASTA DISH, PERFECT FOR AN AL FRESCO MEAL IN SUMMER.
SERVE IT AS A MAIN COURSE LUNCH WITH WARM ITALIAN BREAD AND A DRY WHITE WINE.

SERVES 4

INGREDIENTS

300g/11oz salmon fillet
200ml/7fl oz/scant 1 cup dry
    white wine
a few fresh basil sprigs, plus extra
    basil leaves, to garnish
6 ripe Italian plum tomatoes,
    peeled and finely chopped
150ml/¼ pint/⅔ cup double
    (heavy) cream
350g/12oz/3 cups fresh or
    dried spaghetti
115g/4oz/⅔ cup peeled cooked
    prawns (shrimp), thawed and
    thoroughly dried if frozen
salt and ground black pepper

COOK'S TIP
Check the salmon fillet carefully for
small bones when you are flaking the
flesh. Although the salmon is already
filleted, you will always find a few stray
"pin" bones. Pick them out carefully
using tweezers or your fingertips.

1 Put the salmon, skin side up, in a
wide shallow pan. Pour over the wine,
then add the basil. Sprinkle the fish
with salt and pepper. Bring the wine to
the boil, cover the pan and simmer
gently for 5 minutes. Lift the fish out of
the pan and set it aside to cool a little.

2 Add the tomatoes and cream to
the liquid remaining in the pan and
bring to the boil. Stir well, then reduce
the heat and simmer, uncovered, for
10–15 minutes. Meanwhile, cook the
pasta according to the instructions
on the packet.

3 Flake the fish into large chunks,
discarding the skin and any bones.
Add the fish to the sauce with the prawns,
shaking the pan until they are well coated.
Taste the sauce for seasoning.

4 Drain the pasta and put it in a
warmed bowl. Pour the sauce over
the pasta and toss to combine.
Serve immediately, garnished with
fresh basil leaves.

VARIATION
As a zesty alternative, try substituting
one of the lemons for a lime.

TAGLIATELLE <u>WITH</u> SMOKED SALMON

THIS IS A PRETTY PASTA DISH THAT TASTES AS GOOD AS IT LOOKS. THE LIGHT TEXTURE OF THE CUCUMBER PERFECTLY COMPLEMENTS THE SMOKED SALMON AND THE PASTEL COLOURS LOOK VERY ATTRACTIVE AGAINST THE CREAMY SWIRLS OF TAGLIATELLE.

SERVES 4

INGREDIENTS
  350g/12oz/3 cups dried or
    fresh tagliatelle
  ½ cucumber
  75g/3oz/6 tbsp butter
  grated rind of 1 orange
  30ml/2 tbsp chopped fresh dill
  300ml/½ pint/1¼ cups single
    (light) cream
  15ml/1 tbsp orange juice
  115g/4oz smoked salmon, skinned
  salt and ground black pepper

COOK'S TIP
If the cost of smoked salmon deters you from using it too often, consider buying salmon pieces or off-cuts. These aren't inferior in any way, but because they are either too small or too awkwardly shaped to look good in a packet, they are much cheaper than the neater slices.

1 Bring a large pan of salted water to the boil and add the pasta. If using dried pasta, cook for the time recommended on the packet. If using fresh pasta, cook for 2–3 minutes, or until just tender but still firm to the bite.

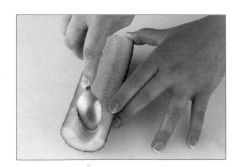

2 Using a sharp knife, cut the cucumber in half lengthways, then use a small spoon to scoop out the cucumber seeds. Turn the cucumber on to the flat side and slice it thinly in crescent shapes.

3 Melt the butter in a heavy pan, add the grated orange rind and fresh chopped dill and stir well to combine. Add the prepared cucumber and cook over a low heat for around 2 minutes, stirring from time to time with a wooden spoon.

4 Stir in the cream and orange juice, then season salt and pepper to taste. Reduce the heat to the lowest setting and cook gently for 1 minute.

5 Cut the smoked salmon into thin even strips. Stir these into the sauce and heat through.

6 Drain the pasta thoroughly in a colander (sieve) and return it to the pan. Add the sauce and toss with a pair of wooden spoons until combined. Spoon into a dish or into individual shallow pasta plates and serve.

CREAMY LEMON AND SALMON PAPPARDELLE

THIS IS A FANTASTIC ALL-IN-ONE SUPPER DISH THAT TASTES GREAT AND IS MADE IN JUST A FEW MINUTES — IDEAL FOR WHEN YOU'RE REALLY HUNGRY BUT HAVEN'T MUCH TIME. SERVE IT WITH A ROCKET SALAD DRESSED WITH EXTRA VIRGIN OLIVE OIL, BALSAMIC VINEGAR AND BLACK PEPPER.

SERVES 4

INGREDIENTS
500g/1¼lb fresh pappardelle
  or tagliatelle
300ml/½ pint/1¼ cups single
  (light) cream
grated rind and juice of 2 lemons
225g/8oz smoked salmon pieces
2.5ml/½ tsp grated nutmeg
60ml/4 tbsp chopped fresh parsley
salt and ground black pepper
Parmesan cheese shavings,
  to garnish
rocket (arugula) salad, to serve

1 Bring a large pan of lightly salted water to the boil and cook the pappardelle or tagliatelle for 3–5 minutes, or according to the instructions on the packet, until risen to the surface of the boiling water and just tender. Drain well.

2 Add the cream, lemon rind and juice to the pan and heat through gently until piping hot. Return the cooked pappardelle to the pan and stir thoroughly to coat the pasta with the creamy mixture.

3 Add the salmon pieces, grated nutmeg, chopped parsley and plenty of ground black pepper to the sauce in the pan and stir well to combine.

4 Divide the pasta among four warmed serving plates and top with the Parmesan shavings. Serve immediately with the rocket salad.

SALMON KEBABS WITH COCONUT

INSPIRED BY FLAVOURS FROM THE WEST INDIES, THIS RECIPE COMBINES COCONUT AND LIME TO PROVIDE A COUNTERPOINT TO THE SUBTLE TASTE OF SALMON AND SCALLOPS.

SERVES 6

INGREDIENTS
   450g/1lb salmon fillet, skinned
   1 small fresh coconut
   2 limes
   12 scallops
   45ml/3 tbsp freshly squeezed
      lime juice
   30ml/2 tbsp soy sauce
   30ml/2 tbsp clear honey
   15ml/1 tbsp soft light
      brown sugar
   ground black pepper

1 Using a sharp knife, cut the salmon into bitesize chunks and place these in a shallow bowl.

2 Halve the coconut and pour the liquor into a jug (pitcher). Using a small, sharp knife, remove the coconut flesh from the inside of the shell and cut it into chunks, making them about the same size as the salmon.

3 Cut each lime into six thick slices. Thread the coconut, salmon, scallops and lime alternately on to six pre-soaked skewers and set aside.

4 Add the lime juice, soy sauce, honey and sugar to the coconut liquor to make the marinade. Mix well and stir in some pepper. You will probably not need salt with the soy sauce.

5 Place the prepared kebabs in a single layer in a shallow non-metallic dish. Pour the marinade over. Cover and chill for at least 3 hours.

6 Place the kebabs on a grill pan. Grill (broil) for 4 minutes on each side, occasionally basting with the marinade.

COOK'S TIP
The easiest way to open a coconut is to carefully hit the fault line with the blunt side of a cleaver. The fault line is situated just between the coconut's "eyes". If done correctly the coconut should split in two.

SALMON WITH TROPICAL FRUIT SALSA

FRESH SALMON, COOKED ON THE BARBECUE, IS GOOD ENOUGH TO SERVE ON ITS OWN, BUT TASTES EVEN BETTER WITH THIS COLOURFUL AND TASTY COMBINATION OF MANGO, PAPAYA AND CHILLI.

SERVES 4

INGREDIENTS

    4 salmon steaks or fillets,
      each about 175g/6oz
    finely grated rind and juice
      of 1 lime
    1 small, ripe mango
    1 small, ripe papaya
    1 fresh red chilli
    45ml/3 tbsp chopped fresh
      coriander (cilantro)
    salt and ground black pepper

COOK'S TIP
If fresh red chillies are not available, use about 2.5ml/½ tsp of chilli paste from a jar, or add a dash of chilli sauce.

1 Lay the pieces of salmon side by side in a wide dish and sprinkle over half the lime rind and juice. Season well.

2 Take a thick slice off either side of the mango stone (pit), and then remove the stone. Finely chop the mango flesh and put it in a bowl. Halve the papaya, scoop out and discard the seeds and remove the skin. Chop the flesh finely and add it to the mango.

3 Cut the chilli in half lengthways. For a milder flavour, remove the seeds, or leave the seeds in to make the salsa hot and spicy. Finely chop the chilli and add to the chopped fruit. Add the chopped fresh coriander to the bowl and mix gently with a large spoon.

4 Stir in the remaining lime rind and juice. Season to taste.

5 Cook the salmon on an oiled barbecue grill over medium-hot coals for 5–8 minutes, turning once. Serve with the tropical fruit salsa.

MAIN DISHES

We should be eating oily fish like salmon and trout at least two or three times a week, but although many of us intend to do just that, we sometimes get stuck in a recipe rut. There's a limit to how many times a person can serve fisherman's pie or grilled salmon, so this chapter introduces some delicious new recipes to expand your repertoire. Dishes like Herby Salmon Parcels, Coconut Salmon, and Salmon with Stilton are easy to prepare and taste great.

CLASSIC FISH PIE

ORIGINALLY A FISH PIE WAS BASED ON THE "CATCH OF THE DAY". SALMON WAS SELDOM INCLUDED, AS IT WAS TOO EXPENSIVE. NOW THAT GOOD QUALITY FARMED SALMON IS AVAILABLE — AND AFFORDABLE — IT MAKES AN EXCELLENT ADDITION TO THE OTHER FISH USED.

SERVES 4

INGREDIENTS
butter, for greasing
450g/1lb mixed fish, including
  salmon fillets
finely grated rind of 1 lemon
450g/1lb floury potatoes, peeled
25g/1oz/2 tbsp butter
salt and ground black pepper
1 egg, beaten

For the sauce
15g/½oz/1 tbsp butter
15ml/1 tbsp plain (all-purpose) flour
150ml/¼ pint/⅔ cup milk
45ml/3 tbsp chopped fresh parsley

1 Preheat the oven to 220°C/425°F/ Gas 7. Grease a baking dish and set aside. Cut the fish into bitesize pieces. Season the fish, sprinkle over the lemon rind and place in the base of the prepared dish.

2 Put the potatoes in a pan. Add cold water to cover and bring to the boil. Cook for 25–30 minutes until tender.

3 Meanwhile, make the sauce. Melt the butter in a pan, add the flour and cook, stirring, for 2–3 minutes. Gradually add the milk, whisking constantly until the mixture boils and thickens to make a smooth white sauce.

4 Stir in the parsley and season to taste. Pour over the fish and mix gently.

5 Drain the potatoes well, return to the pan and mash with the butter.

6 Pipe or spoon the mashed potato on top of the fish mixture. Brush with the beaten egg. Bake for 45 minutes until the potato topping is golden brown. Serve hot.

COOK'S TIP
If using frozen fish thaw it very well and drain it thoroughly, as excess water will ruin the pie.

SEAFOOD LASAGNE

THIS DISH CAN BE AS SIMPLE OR AS ELEGANT AS YOU LIKE. FOR A DINNER PARTY, DRESS IT UP WITH SCALLOPS, MUSSELS OR PRAWNS AND A REALLY GENEROUS PINCH OF SAFFRON IN THE SAUCE; FOR A FAMILY SUPPER, USE SIMPLE FISH SUCH AS COD AND SMOKED HADDOCK.

SERVES 8

INGREDIENTS
  350g/12oz monkfish
  350g/12oz salmon fillet
  350g/12oz undyed smoked haddock
  1 litre/1¾ pints/4 cups milk
  500ml/17fl oz/2¼ cups fish stock
  2 bay leaves or a good pinch of
    saffron threads
  1 small onion, halved
  75g/3oz/6 tbsp butter, plus extra
    for greasing
  45ml/3 tbsp plain (all-purpose) flour
  150g/5oz/2 cups mushrooms,
    sliced
  225–300g/8–11oz no pre-cook or
    fresh lasagne
  60ml/4 tbsp freshly grated
    Parmesan cheese
  salt, ground black pepper, grated
    nutmeg and paprika
  rocket (arugula) leaves,
    to garnish

For the tomato sauce
  30ml/2 tbsp olive oil
  1 red onion, finely chopped
  1 garlic clove, finely chopped
  400g/14oz can chopped tomatoes
  15ml/1 tbsp tomato purée (paste)
  15ml/1 tbsp torn fresh basil leaves

1 Make the tomato sauce. Heat the oil in a pan and fry the onion and garlic over a low heat for 5 minutes, until softened and golden. Stir in the tomatoes and tomato purée and simmer for 20–30 minutes, stirring occasionally. Season and stir in the basil.

2 Put all the fish in a shallow flameproof dish or pan with the milk, stock, bay leaves or saffron and onion. Bring to the boil over a medium heat; poach for 5 minutes, until almost cooked. When the fish is almost cold, lift it out of the pan and place on a board. Strain the liquid and reserve it. Remove skin and any bones, then flake the fish with a fork.

3 Preheat the oven to 180°C/350°F/ Gas 4. Melt the butter in a pan and stir in the flour. Cook for 2 minutes, stirring. Gradually add the poaching liquid and bring to the boil, stirring. Stir in the mushrooms. Cook for 2–3 minutes, then season with salt, pepper and nutmeg.

4 Grease a shallow ovenproof dish. Spoon a thin layer of the mushroom sauce into the dish and spread it with a spatula. Stir the fish into the remaining mushroom sauce in the pan.

5 Add a layer of lasagne, then a layer of fish and sauce. Add another layer of lasagne, then spread over all the tomato sauce. Continue to layer the lasagne and fish, finishing with a final layer of fish and sauce.

6 Sprinkle over the Parmesan cheese. Bake for 30–45 minutes, until golden. Remove from the oven and leave to stand for 10 minutes. Sprinkle with paprika. Garnish with rocket leaves and serve.

SALMON <u>WITH</u> GREEN PEPPERCORNS

SALMON BENEFITS FROM BEING SERVED WITH A PIQUANT ACCOMPANIMENT. LEMON AND LIME ARE THE OBVIOUS CHOICES, BUT CAPERS AND GREEN PEPPERCORNS ALSO SERVE TO COUNTER THE RICH TASTE.

SERVES 4

INGREDIENTS

   15g/½oz/1 tbsp butter
   2–3 shallots, finely chopped
   15ml/1 tbsp brandy (optional)
   60ml/4 tbsp white wine
   90ml/6 tbsp fish or chicken stock
   120ml/4fl oz/½ cup whipping cream
   30–45ml/2–3 tbsp green peppercorns
    in brine, rinsed
   15–30ml/1–2 tbsp vegetable oil
   4 pieces salmon fillet, each about
    175g/6oz
   salt and ground black pepper
   fresh parsley, to garnish

1 Melt the butter in a heavy pan over a medium heat. Add the shallots and cook for 1–2 minutes, until just softened but not coloured.

2 Add the brandy, if using, then pour in the white wine and stock. Bring to the boil. Boil vigorously to reduce by three-quarters, stirring occasionally.

3 Reduce the heat, then add the cream and half the peppercorns, crushing them slightly against the sides of the pan with the back of a spoon. Cook over a very gentle heat for 4–5 minutes, until the sauce has thickened slightly, and coats the back of the spoon.

4 Push the sauce through a sieve (strainer) to remove the peppercorns. Pour into a clean pan and stir in the remaining peppercorns. Keep the sauce warm over a very low heat, stirring occasionally to stop it sticking, while you cook the salmon fillets.

5 Heat the oil in a large, heavy frying pan over a medium-high heat. Lightly season the salmon. When the oil is very hot, add the salmon. Sear the fillets on both sides, then lower the heat and cook for 4–6 minutes, until the flesh is opaque throughout. Arrange the fish on warmed plates and pour over the sauce. Garnish with parsley and serve.

COOK'S TIP
Green peppercorns are available pickled in jars or cans. Keep them on hand for adding to all kinds of sauces and stews. Rinse the peppercorns before use.

PAN-FRIED SALMON WITH MUSHROOM SAUCE

TARRAGON HAS A DISTINCTIVE ANISEED FLAVOUR THAT IS GREAT WITH SALMON. HERE IT IS USED, NOT WITH THE FISH, BUT IN THE EXQUISITE WILD AND FRESH MUSHROOM SAUCE THAT ACCOMPANIES IT.

SERVES 4

INGREDIENTS

50g/2oz/¼ cup butter
salt and cayenne pepper
4 salmon steaks, each 175g/6oz
1 shallot, finely chopped
175g/6oz/about 2½ cups assorted
  wild and cultivated mushrooms,
  trimmed and sliced
200ml/7fl oz/scant 1 cup chicken
  or vegetable stock
10ml/2 tsp cornflour (cornstarch)
2.5ml/½ tsp mustard powder
15ml/1 tbsp water
50ml/3½ tbsp sour cream
45ml/3 tbsp chopped fresh tarragon
5ml/1 tsp white wine vinegar

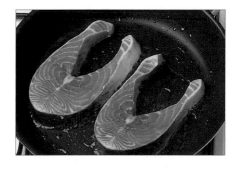

1 Melt half the butter in a large frying pan. Season the salmon, add the steaks to the pan and cook, in batches if necessary, over a medium heat for 8 minutes, turning once. Transfer to a plate, cover and keep warm.

2 Heat the remaining butter in the pan and gently fry the shallot until softened but not coloured. Add the mushrooms and cook until the juices begin to flow.

3 Add the stock and simmer for 2–3 minutes. Put the cornflour and mustard powder in a cup and mix to a paste with the water. Stir into the mushroom mixture and bring to a simmer, stirring until the sauce thickens. Stir in the sour cream, tarragon and vinegar. Season the sauce with salt and cayenne pepper.

4 Spoon the mushroom sauce over each salmon steak and serve with new potatoes and a green salad.

COOK'S TIP
Fresh tarragon will bruise and darken quickly after it is chopped. To avoid this try to prepare the herb just before you are ready to use it.

SALMON WITH WHISKY AND CREAM

THIS DISH COMBINES TWO OF THE FINEST FLAVOURS OF SCOTLAND – SALMON AND WHISKY. IT TAKES VERY LITTLE TIME TO MAKE, SO COOK IT AT THE LAST MOMENT. SERVE QUITE PLAINLY, ACCOMPANIED BY BEAUTIFULLY SOFT NEW POTATOES AND CRUNCHY GREEN BEANS.

SERVES 4

INGREDIENTS

    4 thin pieces of salmon fillet, about
      175g/6oz each
    5ml/1 tsp chopped fresh
      thyme leaves
    50g/2oz/¼ cup butter
    75ml/5 tbsp whisky
    150ml/¼ pint/⅔ cup double
      (heavy) cream
    juice of ½ lemon (optional)
    salt and ground black pepper
    fresh dill sprigs, to garnish

VARIATION
For a non-alcoholic, but equally tasty, alternative, try omitting the whisky and stirring a handful of chopped tarragon into the sauce alongside the lemon juice.

1 Season the salmon with salt, pepper and thyme. Melt half the butter in a frying pan large enough to hold two pieces of salmon side by side.

2 When the butter is foaming, fry the first two pieces of salmon for 2–3 minutes on each side, until they are golden on the outside and just cooked through.

3 Pour in 30ml/2 tbsp of the whisky and ignite it. When the flames have died down, carefully transfer the salmon to a plate and keep it hot. Heat the remaining butter and cook the second two pieces of salmon in the same way. Keep them hot.

4 Pour the cream into the pan and bring to the boil, stirring constantly and scraping up the cooking juices from the base of the pan. Allow to bubble until reduced and slightly thickened, then season and add the last of the whisky and a squeeze of lemon if you like.

5 Place the salmon pieces on individual warmed plates, pour the sauce over and garnish with dill. New potatoes and crisp green beans are good with this.

SALMON WITH STILTON

A RICH BLUE STILTON AND HERB BUTTER MAKES A FLAVOURSOME SAUCE FOR SALMON STEAKS BAKED IN WINE. SERVE THIS TOTALLY MOUTHWATERING MELANGE WITH STEAMING NEW POTATOES, STIR-FRIED RED AND YELLOW PEPPERS AND CRUNCHY MANGETOUTS.

SERVES 4

INGREDIENTS
115g/4oz Stilton cheese
25g/1oz/2 tbsp butter, softened
15ml/1 tbsp chopped fresh chives, plus extra, to garnish
15ml/1 tbsp chopped fresh thyme leaves
1 garlic clove, crushed
30ml/2 tbsp olive oil
4 salmon steaks
60ml/4 tbsp dry white wine
salt and ground black pepper
new potatoes and stir-fried red and yellow (bell) peppers and mangetouts (snow peas), to serve

1 Crumble the Stilton and place it in a food processor with the butter. Process until smooth. Scrape the mixture into a small mixing bowl.

2 Stir the chives, thyme and garlic into the stilton and butter mixture. Season to taste. Stilton is salty, so you will probably only need to add pepper. Preheat the oven to 180°C/350°F/Gas 4.

3 Place the butter on a piece of foil and shape into an oblong. Wrap this in the foil and seal tightly. Chill the butter in the refrigerator until it is firm.

4 Brush a sheet of foil, large enough to enclose all the steaks, with olive oil. Place the steaks on the foil, drizzle the wine over, season and seal the foil tightly. Bake for 20–30 minutes or until cooked through.

5 Unwrap the chilled butter and cut it into four equal portions. Remove the salmon from the oven, carefully open the package and use a fish slice (metal spatula) to transfer each steak to a warmed serving plate.

6 Top each salmon steak with a portion of the stilton butter and garnish with the extra chives. Serve immediately, while the butter is just starting to melt over the salmon, accompanied with steaming hot new potatoes and stir-fried red and yellow peppers and crunchy mangetouts.

COOK'S TIPS
• If your food processor has a mini bowl for small quantities, use that when making the Stilton butter.
• When wrapping the salmon steaks, turn the foil joins over twice to make a tight seal. This will ensure that the salmon cooks evenly.

SALMON WITH ROASTED VEGETABLES

THIS COLOURFUL AND TASTY DISH IS PERFECT FOR A SUMMER MEAL, AND BECAUSE IT IS SO EASY TO COOK, YOU DON'T HAVE TO SPEND TIME IN THE KITCHEN WHEN YOU COULD BE SOAKING UP THE SUN.

3 Place the salmon fillets in a single layer in a roasting pan. Pour over the lemon juice and olive oil. Turn the salmon fillets to coat them in the mixture. Season with salt and pepper.

4 Spoon the vegetable mixture into a separate roasting pan. Set aside eight basil leaves for the garnish, and tuck the rest among the vegetables.

5 Place both roasting pans in the oven, with the vegetables on a higher shelf than the fish. Bake for about 15 minutes or until the fish is opaque and the vegetables are just beginning to char at the edges.

6 To serve, arrange the vegetables on four serving plates. Top each portion with a salmon fillet and garnish with the reserved basil leaves. Serve with walnut bread and olive oil for dipping.

VARIATIONS
• This dish works equally well with fillets of tuna or cod.
• For a mediterranean feel, try scattering some sun-dried tomatoes in with the vegetables before cooking.

SERVES 4

INGREDIENTS
  175g/6oz green beans, trimmed
  1 red (bell) pepper, seeded
    and sliced
  1 yellow (bell) pepper, seeded
    and sliced
  16 cherry tomatoes, halved
  50g/2oz/½ cup pitted
    black olives
  50g/2oz/½ cup pitted
    green olives
  30ml/2 tbsp garlic-flavoured olive oil
  4 salmon fillets, each about
    200g/7oz
  juice of ½ lemon
  30ml/2 tbsp olive oil
  1 bunch fresh basil, leaves stripped
    from stems
  salt and ground black pepper
  walnut bread and olive oil, to serve

1 Preheat the oven to 220°C/425°F/ Gas 7. Bring a pan of lightly salted water to the boil. Add the trimmed green beans and cook them over a medium heat until they are just tender.

2 Drain the green beans very well, then put them into a large bowl. Add the red and yellow peppers, the tomatoes and the olives. Season well, drizzle the garlic oil over and stir to coat.

SALMON BAKED <u>WITH</u> POTATOES <u>AND</u> THYME

THIS IS VERY SIMPLE AND ABSOLUTELY DELICIOUS. PEPPER-CRUSTED SALMON FILLETS ARE BAKED ON A BED OF POTATOES AND ONIONS BRAISED IN THYME-FLAVOURED VEGETABLE OR FISH STOCK.

SERVES 4

INGREDIENTS

675g/1½lb waxy potatoes, thinly sliced
1 onion, thinly sliced
10ml/2 tsp fresh thyme leaves
450ml/¾ pint/scant 2 cups vegetable or fish stock
40g/1½oz/3 tbsp butter, finely diced
4 salmon fillets, each about 150g/5oz, skinned
30ml/2 tbsp olive oil
15ml/1 tbsp black peppercorns, roughly crushed
salt and ground black pepper
fresh thyme, to garnish
mangetouts (snow peas) or sugar snap peas, to serve

COOK'S TIP

A mandolin can be used to achieve perfect, thinly-sliced potatoes.

1 Preheat the oven to 190°C/375°F/ Gas 5. Layer the potato and onion slices in a shallow baking dish, such as a lasagne dish, seasoning each layer and sprinkling with thyme. Pour over the stock, dot with butter, cover with foil and place in the oven.

2 Bake the potatoes for 40 minutes then remove the foil and bake for a further 20 minutes, or until they are almost cooked.

3 Meanwhile brush the salmon fillets with olive oil and coat with crushed black peppercorns, pressing them in, if necessary, with the back of a spoon.

4 Place the salmon on top of the potatoes, cover with foil and bake for 15 minutes, or until the salmon is opaque, removing the foil for the last 5 minutes. Garnish with fresh thyme sprigs and serve with mangetouts or sugar snap peas.

SALMON AND BLACK-EYED BEAN STEW

THE ADDITION OF FRESH SALMON TO THIS STEW HELPS TO MAKE IT AN EXTREMELY NOURISHING DISH, AS WELL AS A DELICIOUS WINTER WARMER. THE CANNED BEANS ARE AN ADDED ENERGY BOOST.

SERVES 2

INGREDIENTS
   150g/5oz salmon fillet, skinned and
      any bones removed
   400g/14oz canned black-eyed beans
      (peas) in brine
   50g/2oz fresh shiitake mushrooms,
      stalks removed
   1 small carrot, peeled
   ½ mooli (daikon), peeled
   5g/⅛oz dashi-konbu (dried kelp
      seaweed), about 10cm/4in square
   60ml/4 tbsp water
   15ml/1 tbsp shoyu (Japanese
      soy sauce)
   7.5ml/1½ tsp mirin or dry sherry
   sea salt
   2.5cm/1in fresh root ginger, peeled,
      to garnish

COOK'S TIP
Dried black-eyed beans (peas) can
also be used, but must be soaked in
water for at least 8 hours first.

1 Slice the salmon into 1cm/½in-thick strips. Place in a colander, sprinkle with sea salt and leave for 1 hour.

2 Wash away the salt and cut the salmon strips into 1cm/½in cubes. Par-boil in a pan of rapidly boiling water for 30 seconds, then drain. Gently rinse under cold running water to prevent the cubes from cooking further.

3 Slice the ginger for the garnish thinly lengthways, then stack the slices and cut them into thin threads. Soak in cold water for about 30 minutes, then drain well.

4 Drain the can of black-eyed beans into a medium pan. Reserve the beans.

5 Chop all the fresh vegetables into 1cm/½in cubes. Wipe the dashi-konbu with kitchen paper, then snip with scissors. Cut everything as close to the same size as possible.

6 Put the par-boiled salmon, dashi-konbu and vegetables into the pan containing the liquid from the can of beans. Pour the beans on top and add the 60ml/4 tbsp water and 1.5ml/¼ tsp salt. Bring to the boil. Reduce the heat to low and cook for 6 minutes or until the carrot is cooked.

7 Add the shoyu and cook for a further 4 minutes. Add the mirin or sherry and remove the pan from the heat. Mix well. Leave to rest for 1 hour. Serve warm or cold, with the ginger threads.

SALMON COULIBIAC

THIS IS A COMPLICATED RUSSIAN DISH THAT TAKES A LOT OF PREPARATION, BUT IT IS WELL WORTH IT. TRADITIONALLY, STURGEON IS USED, BUT SALMON MAKES AN EXCELLENT ALTERNATIVE.

SERVES 8

INGREDIENTS
  butter, for greasing
  flour, for dusting
  450g/1lb puff pastry
  1 egg, beaten
  salt and ground black pepper
  lemon wedges and fresh dill sprigs,
    to garnish

For the filling
  50g/2oz/¼ cup butter
  350g/12oz/5 cups chestnut
    mushrooms, sliced
  105ml/7 tbsp white wine
  juice of ½ lemon
  675g/1½lb salmon
    fillet, skinned
  115g/4oz/scant ½ cup
    long grain rice
  30ml/2 tbsp chopped fresh dill
  1 large onion, chopped
  4 hard-boiled eggs, shelled
    and sliced

1 First make the filling. Melt most of the butter in a frying pan that is large enough to accommodate the salmon. Add the mushrooms and cook for 3 minutes. Pour in 60ml/4 tbsp of the wine and boil for 2 minutes, then simmer for 5 minutes. Stir in almost all of the remaining wine and the lemon juice.

2 Place the salmon on top of the cooked mushrooms, cover with foil and steam gently for 8–10 minutes, until just cooked. Remove the salmon from the pan and set aside.

3 With a slotted spoon, transfer the mushrooms to a bowl. Pour the cooking liquid into a large pan. Add the rice and cook for 10–15 minutes, until tender, adding water or more wine if needed.

4 Remove from the heat and stir in the dill and seasoning. Melt the remaining butter and fry the onion until golden brown. Set aside.

5 Grease a large baking sheet. Cut out a fish-shaped template with baking parchment, that will fit easily on the baking sheet. Roll out just less than half the pastry and use the template to cut a fish shape. Place on the baking sheet.

6 Leaving the edges clear, spread half the mushrooms on the pastry and top with half the rice, onion and eggs. Place the salmon on top, cutting it to fit if needed, then repeat the layers in reverse.

7 Roll out the remaining pastry and cut a slightly larger fish shape than before. Brush the base pastry rim with beaten egg, fit the pastry top in place and seal the edges. Chill for 1 hour.

8 Preheat the oven to 220°C/425°F/ Gas 7. Cut four small slits in the top of the pastry, brush with more egg and bake for 10 minutes. Reduce the oven temperature to 190°C/375°F/Gas 5 and bake for 30 minutes more, until golden. Garnish with lemon and dill and serve.

SALMON AND RICE GRATIN

THIS ALL-IN-ONE SUPPER DISH IS IDEAL FOR INFORMAL ENTERTAINING AS IT CAN BE MADE AHEAD OF TIME AND REHEATED FOR ABOUT HALF AN HOUR BEFORE BEING SERVED WITH A TOSSED SALAD.

SERVES 6

INGREDIENTS

675g/1½lb fresh salmon fillet, skinned
1 bay leaf
a few parsley stalks
1 litre/1¾ pints/4 cups water
400g/14oz/2 cups basmati rice,
  soaked in cold water for 30 minutes
30–45ml/2–3 tbsp chopped fresh
  parsley, plus extra to garnish
175g/6oz/1½ cups grated
  Cheddar cheese
3 hard-boiled eggs, chopped
salt and ground black pepper

For the sauce
1 litre/1¾ pints/4 cups milk
40g/1½oz/⅓ cup plain
  (all-purpose) flour
40g/1½oz/3 tbsp butter
5ml/1 tsp mild curry paste or
  Dijon mustard

4 Remove the pan from the heat and, without lifting the lid, allow the rice to stand undisturbed for 5 minutes.

5 Meanwhile, make the sauce. Mix the milk, flour and butter in a pan. Bring to the boil over a low heat, whisking constantly until the sauce is smooth and thick. Stir in the curry paste or mustard, with salt and pepper to taste. Reduce the heat and simmer the sauce for 2 minutes, whisking occasionally.

6 Preheat the grill (broiler). Remove the sauce from the heat and stir in the chopped parsley and rice, with half the cheese. Using a large metal spoon, fold in the flaked fish and eggs.

7 Spoon into a shallow gratin dish and sprinkle with the rest of the cheese. Heat under the grill until the topping is golden brown and bubbling. Serve in individual dishes, garnished with chopped parsley.

1 Put the salmon in a wide, shallow pan. Add the bay leaf and parsley stalks, with salt and pepper. Pour in the water and bring to simmering point. Poach the fish for about 12 minutes until just tender.

2 Lift the fish out of the pan using a slotted spoon, then strain the liquid into a clean pan. Leave the fish to cool, then remove any visible bones and flake the flesh gently with a fork.

3 Drain the rice and add it to the pan containing the fish-poaching liquid. Bring to the boil, then reduce the heat, cover and simmer for 10 minutes.

SALMON <u>WITH</u> SPICY PESTO

THIS IS A GREAT WAY TO BONE SALMON STEAKS TO GIVE A SOLID PIECE OF FISH. THE PESTO USES SUNFLOWER KERNELS AND CHILLI AS ITS FLAVOURING RATHER THAN THE CLASSIC BASIL AND PINE NUTS.

SERVES 4

INGREDIENTS

    4 salmon steaks, each about 225g/8oz
    30ml/2 tbsp sunflower oil
    finely grated rind and juice of 1 lime
    salt and ground black pepper

For the pesto
    6 fresh mild red chillies, seeded and
      roughly chopped
    2 garlic cloves
    30ml/2 tbsp pumpkin or
      sunflower seeds
    finely grated rind and juice of 1 lime
    75ml/5 tbsp olive oil

1 Place a salmon steak flat on a board. Insert a very sharp knife close to the top of the bone. Staying close to the bone all the time, cut to the end of the steak to release one side of the steak. Repeat with the other side.

2 Place one piece of salmon skin side down and hold it firmly with one hand. Insert a small sharp knife under the skin and, working away from you, cut the flesh off in a single piece. Repeat with the remaining salmon steaks.

3 Wrap each piece of fish into a circle, with the thinner end wrapped around the fatter end. Tie with string (twine). Place in a shallow bowl.

4 Rub the oil into the boneless fish rounds. Add the lime juice and rind to the bowl. Cover and marinate in the refrigerator for 2 hours.

5 Make the pesto. Put the chillies, garlic, pumpkin or sunflower seeds, lime rind and juice and seasoning into a food processor. Process until well mixed. With the machine running, gradually add the olive oil through the feeder tube. The pesto will slowly thicken and emulsify. Scrape it into a bowl. Preheat the grill (broiler).

6 Drain the salmon and place the rounds in a grill pan. Grill (broil) for 5 minutes on each side or until opaque. Serve with the spicy pesto.

COOK'S TIP

If any small bones remain in the salmon steaks after preparation, remove them with fish tweezers or a pair of new eyebrow tweezers kept for the purpose.

HERBY SALMON PARCELS

COOKING SALMON, OR ANY FISH, IN A PARCEL HELPS TO KEEP IT MOIST AND SEALS IN ALL THE WONDERFUL FLAVOURS. LIME AND BASIL GIVE THE FISH A FRESH, TANGY TASTE.

SERVES 4

INGREDIENTS
   1 lime
   50g/2oz/¼ cup butter,
     softened
   30ml/2 tbsp finely chopped
     fresh basil
   4 plum tomatoes, sliced
   2 garlic cloves, thinly
     sliced
   4 salmon fillets, each about
     200g/7oz
   15ml/1 tbsp olive oil
   salt and black pepper

1 Grate the rind from the lime and put it in a small bowl. Cut the lime into eight slices and set aside. Add the butter and basil to the lime rind and mix well.

2 Roll the butter mixture into a cylindrical shape, wrap in greaseproof (waxed) paper or baking parchment and chill in the refrigerator.

3 Preheat the oven to 190°C/375°F/ Gas 5. Cut out sheets of greaseproof paper or baking parchment, each large enough to enclose a salmon fillet easily.

4 Arrange one whole sliced tomato in the centre of each piece of paper or parchment. Sprinkle each sliced tomato with one-quarter of the sliced garlic and season with plenty of salt and pepper.

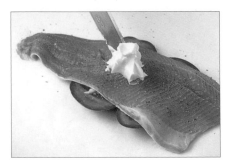

5 Place one salmon fillet on each pile of tomatoes and garlic. Cut the chilled, flavoured butter into four equally-sized pieces and place one on each salmon fillet. Top each piece of salmon with two of the reserved lime slices and drizzle evenly with the olive oil.

6 Fold the paper or parchment around the topped salmon to make neat parcels, making sure that each parcel is firmly secured at the edges so that no juices will escape during cooking. Place the parcels on a baking sheet and bake for 20 minutes or until the fish is cooked through.

COOK'S TIP
The flavour of the tomatoes is central to the success of this dish. If you can obtain home-grown Italian plum tomatoes, such as San Morzano, so much the better. Alternatively, go for sweet and juicy cherry tomatoes.

SALMON IN A LEAF PARCEL

THIS IS AN INDIAN SPECIALITY FROM MUMBAI – OR, TO USE THE OLD NAME, BOMBAY. THERE IT WOULD BE MADE USING SILVER POMFRET, BUT SALMON, WITH ITS ROBUST FLAVOUR, ALSO WORKS WELL.

SERVES 6

INGREDIENTS

50g/2oz fresh coconut, skinned and finely grated, or 65g/2½oz/scant 1 cup desiccated (dry unsweetened shredded) coconut, soaked in 30ml/2 tbsp water

1 large lemon, skin, pith and seeds removed, roughly chopped

4 large garlic cloves, crushed

3 large fresh mild green chillies, seeded and chopped

50g/2oz/1 cup fresh coriander (cilantro), roughly chopped

25g/1oz/½ cup fresh mint leaves, roughly chopped

5ml/1 tsp ground cumin

5ml/1 tsp sugar

2.5ml/½ tsp fenugreek seeds, finely ground

5ml/1 tsp salt

2 large, whole banana leaves

6 salmon fillets, total weight about 1.2kg/2½lb, skinned

1 Place all the ingredients except the banana leaves and salmon in a food processor. Pulse to a fine paste. Scrape the mixture into a bowl, cover and chill for 30 minutes.

2 Make the parcels. Cut each banana leaf widthways into three and cut off the hard outside edge from each piece. Put the pieces of leaf and the edge strips in a bowl of hot water. Leave to soak for about 10 minutes.

3 Drain the leaf pieces and strips and gently wipe off any white residue. Rinse and pour over boiling water to soften. Drain again, then place the leaf pieces and strips, smooth side up, on a clean board to dry.

COOK'S TIP

Serve little rice parcels with the salmon. Fill six more banana leaf packages with cooked basmati rice, secure each one with a skewer and reheat on the grill.

4 Smear the top and bottom of each leaf with the coconut paste. Place one salmon fillet on each leaf. Bring the trimmed edge of the leaf over the salmon, then fold in the sides. Finally, bring up the remaining edge to cover the salmon and make a neat parcel. Tie each parcel securely with one of the soaked leaf strips.

5 Lay each parcel on a sheet of heavy-duty foil, bring up the edges and scrunch the tops together to seal. Position a lightly oiled grill rack over medium-hot coals to heat. Place the salmon parcels on the grill rack and cook for 10 minutes, turning over once.

6 Place the parcels on a board and leave to stand for 2–3 minutes – the salmon will continue to cook in the residual heat. Remove the foil, then transfer each banana leaf parcel to a plate, to be unwrapped at the table. Eat the fish straight out of the parcel.

HOT SMOKED SALMON

THIS IS A FANTASTIC WAY OF SMOKING SALMON ON A CHARCOAL BARBECUE, USING SOAKED HICKORY WOOD CHIPS THAT IMPART A DELICATE SMOKEY FLAVOUR. MOJO, A SPICY BUT NOT HOT SAUCE POPULAR IN CUBA, IS PERFECT TO CUT THE RICHNESS OF THE HOT SMOKED SALMON.

SERVES 6

INGREDIENTS
    6 salmon fillets, each about
      175g/6oz, with skin
    15ml/1 tbsp sunflower oil
    salt and ground black pepper
    2 handfuls hickory wood chips,
      soaked in cold water for at least
      30 minutes

For the mojo
    1 ripe mango, diced
    4 drained canned pineapple
      slices, diced
    1 small red onion, finely chopped
    1 fresh long mild red chilli, seeded
      and finely chopped
    15ml/1 tbsp good quality sweet
      chilli sauce
    grated rind and juice of 1 lime
    leaves from 1 small lemon basil plant
      or 45ml/3 tbsp fresh coriander
      (cilantro) leaves, chopped

1 Place the salmon fillets, skin side down, on a large platter. Sprinkle the flesh lightly with salt. Cover with clear film (plastic wrap) and leave in a cool place for about 30 minutes.

2 Make the mojo by putting the diced mango and pineapple, chopped onion and seeded and chopped chilli in a mixing bowl.

3 Add the chilli sauce, lime rind and juice, and the chopped herb leaves. Stir to mix well. Cover tightly and leave in a cool place until needed.

4 Pat the salmon fillets with kitchen paper, then brush each one with a little of the sunflower oil. Place the salmon fillets skin side down on a lightly oiled grill rack over medium-hot coals. Cover the barbecue with a lid or tented heavy-duty foil and cook the fish for about 3 minutes.

5 Drain the hickory chips into a colander and sprinkle about a third of them as evenly as possible over the coals. Carefully drop them through the slats in the grill racks, taking care not to scatter the ash as you do so.

6 Replace the barbecue cover and continue cooking for a further 8 minutes, adding a small handful of hickory chips twice more during this time. Serve the salmon hot or cold, with the mojo.

SALMON AND SCALLOP BROCHETTES

USING LEMON GRASS AS SKEWERS ISN'T A CULINARY GIMMICK. THE SUBTLE FLAVOUR GIVES THE
INGREDIENTS — IN THIS CASE, SALMON AND SCALLOPS — A FRAGRANCE THAT SEEMS PERFECTLY IN
KEEPING WITH THE DELICACY OF THIS SUPERB DINNER DISH.

SERVES 4

INGREDIENTS

   8 lemon grass stalks
   225g/8oz salmon fillet, skinned
   8 queen scallops, with their corals
    if possible
   8 baby onions, peeled and blanched
   ½ yellow (bell) pepper, cut into
    eight squares
   100g/4oz/½ cup butter
   juice of ½ lemon
   30ml/2 tbsp dry vermouth
   5ml/1 tsp chopped fresh tarragon
   salt, ground white pepper
    and paprika

COOK'S TIP

Soak the lemon grass stalks in water for
several hours before grilling (broiling).
This will prevent them from burning.

1 Preheat the grill (broiler) to medium-
high. Cut off the top 7.5–10cm/3–4in
of each lemon grass stalk. Reserve the
bulb ends for another dish. Cut the
salmon fillet into twelve 2cm/¾in cubes.
Thread the salmon, scallops, corals if
available, onions and pepper squares
on to the lemon grass sticks and
arrange the brochettes side by side in
a grill (broiler) pan.

2 Melt half the butter in a small pan,
add the lemon juice and a pinch of
paprika and then brush all over the
brochettes. Grill (broil) the skewers
for about 2–3 minutes on each side,
turning and basting the brochettes
every minute, until the fish and scallops
are just cooked, but are still very juicy.
Transfer to a platter and keep hot while
you make the tarragon butter sauce.

3 Pour the dry vermouth and all the
leftover cooking juices from the
brochettes into a small pan and boil
quite fiercely to reduce by half. Add the
remaining butter and melt, stirring all
the time. Stir in the chopped fresh
tarragon and add salt and ground white
pepper to taste. Pour the tarragon
butter sauce over the brochettes and
serve immediately.

MEXICAN BARBECUE SALMON

THESE SALMON FILLETS COOK QUICKLY ON THE BARBECUE, AND BECAUSE THEY'VE BEEN MARINATED IN THE TOMATO SAUCE, THEY REMAIN BEAUTIFULLY MOIST AND SUCCULENT.

SERVES 4

INGREDIENTS

25g/1oz/2 tbsp butter
1 small red onion, finely chopped
1 garlic clove, crushed
6 plum tomatoes, diced
45ml/3 tbsp tomato ketchup
30ml/2 tbsp Dijon mustard
30ml/2 tbsp soft dark brown sugar
15ml/1 tbsp clear honey
5ml/1 tsp ground cayenne pepper
15ml/1 tbsp ancho chilli powder
15ml/1 tbsp paprika
15ml/1 tbsp Worcestershire sauce
4 salmon fillets, each about 175g/6oz
fresh flat leaf parsley sprigs,
  to garnish

3 Add the tomato ketchup, Dijon mustard, brown sugar, honey, cayenne pepper, chilli powder, paprika and Worcestershire sauce. Stir well, then simmer for a further 20 minutes. Pour the mixture into a food processor and process until smooth. Leave to cool.

4 Put the salmon fillets in a shallow dish, brush generously with the sauce and chill for at least 2 hours. Cook the salmon fillets on an oiled barbecue grill over medium-hot coals for 2–3 minutes on each side, brushing frequently with the sauce. Garnish and serve.

1 Melt the butter in a large, heavy pan and cook the onion and garlic gently for about 5 minutes until softened and translucent. Do not let the onion brown.

2 Add the diced plum tomatoes. Bring to the boil, then reduce the heat and simmer for 15 minutes. Stir the tomatoes occasionally with a wooden spoon so that they do not catch on the base of the pan.

ASIAN SEARED SALMON

SALMON FILLETS ONLY TAKE A FEW MINUTES TO COOK, BUT MAKE SURE YOU ALLOW ENOUGH TIME FOR
THE FISH TO SOAK UP ALL THE FLAVOURS OF THE MARINADE BEFORE YOU START COOKING.

SERVES 4

INGREDIENTS
grated rind and juice of 1 lime
15ml/1 tbsp soy sauce
2 spring onions (scallions), sliced
1 fresh red chilli, seeded and
   finely chopped
2.5cm/1in piece fresh root ginger,
   peeled and grated
1 lemon grass stalk, finely chopped
4 salmon fillets, each about
   175g/6oz
30ml/2 tbsp olive oil
salt and ground black pepper
45ml/3 tbsp fresh coriander
   (cilantro), to garnish

For the noodles
250g/9oz medium egg noodles
30ml/2 tbsp olive oil
1 carrot, cut into fine strips
1 red (bell) pepper, seeded and cut
   into fine strips
1 yellow (bell) pepper, seeded and
   cut into fine strips
115g/4oz mangetouts (snow peas)
15ml/1 tbsp sesame oil

1 Put the grated lime rind in a jug (pitcher) and pour in the lime juice. Add the soy sauce, spring onions, chilli, ginger and lemon grass. Season with pepper and stir well. Place the salmon in a shallow non-metallic dish and pour the lime mixture over. Cover and marinate in the refrigerator for at least 30 minutes.

2 Bring a large pan of lightly salted water to the boil and cook the noodles according to the instructions on the packet. Drain well and set aside.

COOK'S TIP
Fresh root ginger is a wonderful ingredient. Thin slices can be added to boiling water to make a refreshing tea, and grated ginger makes a great addition to curries and stir-fries. Ginger freezes successfully and can be shaved or grated from frozen.

3 Brush a griddle pan with 15ml/1 tbsp of the olive oil and heat until hot. Remove the fish from the marinade, pat dry and add to the griddle pan. Cook the salmon fillets for 6 minutes, turning once.

4 When the salmon is almost cooked, add to the remaining marinade in a separate pan and heat through.

5 While the fish is cooking, heat the remaining oil in a wok or large frying pan. Add the carrot and stir-fry for 3 minutes. Add the drained noodles, pepper strips and mangetouts and toss over the heat for 2 minutes more. Drizzle the sesame oil over and season well.

6 Serve the salmon on a bed of noodles and vegetables. Garnish with coriander.

SALMON AND VEGETABLES IN A PARCEL

FOR THIS DELIGHTFUL JAPANESE RECIPE, SALMON IS STEAMED WITH SAKE AND BEAUTIFULLY CARVED VEGETABLES IN A FOIL PARCEL. WHEN THE PARCELS ARE OPENED, THE CONTENTS LOOK LOVELY.

SERVES 4

INGREDIENTS
  500g/1¼lb salmon
    fillet, skinned
  30ml/2 tbsp sake
  15ml/1 tbsp shoyu (Japanese
    soy sauce), plus extra to
    serve (optional)
  about 250g/9oz/3 cups fresh
    shimeji mushrooms
  8 fresh shiitake mushrooms
  2.5cm/1in piece of carrot
  4 spring onions (scallions)
  115g/4oz/1 cup mangetouts
    (snow peas)
  salt

1 Preheat the oven to 190°C/375°F/ Gas 5. Cut the salmon into bitesize pieces. Place in a shallow bowl and add the sake and shoyu. Marinate for about 15 minutes. Drain and reserve the marinade.

2 Clean the shimeji mushrooms and chop off the hard root from each. Remove and discard the stalks from the shiitake. Carve a shallow slit on the top of each shiitake with a sharp knife inserted at a slant. Repeat from the other side to cut out a notch about 4cm/1½in long. Rotate the shiitake 90° and carve another notch to make a small white cross in the brown top.

3 Slice the carrot very thinly, then use a Japanese vegetable cutter or sharp knife to cut out 8–12 maple-leaf or flower shapes. Carefully slice the spring onions in half lengthways with a sharp knife. Trim the mangetouts.

4 Cut four sheets of foil, each about 29 x 21cm/11½ x 8½in. With the long side of one sheet facing you, arrange the salmon and shimeji mushrooms in the centre, then place a spring onion diagonally across them. Put two shiitake on top, three or four mangetouts in a fan shape and then sprinkle with a few carrot shapes.

5 Sprinkle the marinade and a good pinch of salt over the top. Fold the two longer sides of the foil together, then fold the shorter sides to seal. Repeat to make four parcels.

6 Place the parcels on a baking sheet and bake for 15–20 minutes in the middle of the preheated oven. When the foil has expanded into a balloon, the dish is ready to serve. Take the parcels to the table unopened and offer a little extra shoyu, if required.

STIR-FRIED NOODLES WITH SOY SALMON

TERIYAKI SAUCE FORMS THE MARINADE FOR THE SALMON IN THIS RECIPE. SERVED WITH STIR-FRIED NOODLES, IT MAKES A STUNNING DISH.

SERVES 4

INGREDIENTS
- 350g/12oz salmon fillet, skinned
- 30ml/2 tbsp shoyu (Japanese soy sauce)
- 30ml/2 tbsp sake
- 60ml/4 tbsp mirin or sweet sherry
- 5ml/1 tsp soft light brown sugar
- 10ml/2 tsp grated fresh root ginger
- 3 garlic cloves, 1 crushed, and 2 sliced into rounds
- 30ml/2 tbsp groundnut (peanut) oil
- 225g/8oz dried egg noodles, cooked and drained
- 50g/2oz/1 cup alfalfa sprouts
- 30ml/2 tbsp sesame seeds, lightly toasted

1 Using a sharp cook's knife, slice the salmon thinly. Spread out the slices in a large, shallow dish, keeping them in a single layer if possible.

3 Preheat the grill (broiler). Drain the salmon, reserving the marinade. Place the salmon in a layer on a baking sheet. Cook under the grill for 2–3 minutes.

5 Add the cooked noodles and reserved marinade to the wok and stir-fry for 3–4 minutes until the marinade has reduced to a syrupy glaze and coats the noodles.

2 In a bowl, mix together the soy sauce, sake, mirin or sherry, sugar, ginger and crushed garlic. Pour over the salmon, cover and leave for 30 minutes.

4 Meanwhile, heat a wok until hot, add the oil and swirl it around. Add the garlic rounds and cook until golden brown. Remove the garlic and discard.

6 Toss in the alfalfa sprouts. Transfer immediately to warmed serving plates and top with the salmon. Sprinkle over the toasted sesame seeds. Serve at once.

SALMON TERIYAKI

SAKE TERIYAKI IS A WELL-KNOWN JAPANESE DISH, WHICH USES A SWEET AND SHINY SAUCE FOR MARINATING AS WELL AS FOR GLAZING THE INGREDIENTS.

SERVES 4

INGREDIENTS
 4 small salmon fillets with skin on,
   each weighing about 150g/5oz
 50g/2oz/1 cup beansprouts, washed
 50g/2oz mangetouts (snow peas)
 20g/¾oz carrot, cut into thin strips
 salt

For the teriyaki sauce
 45ml/3 tbsp shoyu (Japanese soy sauce)
 45ml/3 tbsp sake
 45ml/3 tbsp mirin or sweet sherry
 15ml/1 tbsp plus 10ml/2 tsp caster
   (superfine) sugar

1 Make the teriyaki sauce. Mix the shoyu, sake, mirin and 15ml/1 tbsp caster sugar in a pan. Heat, stirring, to dissolve the sugar. Cool for 1 hour.

2 Place the salmon fillets, skin side down, in a shallow glass or china dish. Pour over the teriyaki sauce. Leave to marinate for 30 minutes.

3 Meanwhile, bring a pan of lightly salted water to the boil. Add the beansprouts, then after 1 minute, the mangetouts. Leave for 1 minute then add the thin carrot strips. Remove the pan from the heat after 1 minute, then drain the vegetables and keep warm.

4 Preheat the grill (broiler) to medium. Take the salmon fillet out of the sauce and pat dry with kitchen paper. Reserve the sauce. Lightly oil a grilling (broiling) tray. Grill (broil) the salmon for about 6 minutes, turning once, until golden.

5 Meanwhile, pour the remaining teriyaki sauce into a small pan, add the remaining sugar and heat until dissolved. Brush the salmon with the sauce.

6 Continue to grill the salmon until the surface of the fish bubbles. Turn over and repeat on the other side.

7 Heap the vegetables on to serving plates. Place the salmon on top and spoon over the rest of the sauce.

COOK'S TIP
To save time, you could use ready-made teriyaki sauce for the marinade. This useful ingredient comes in bottles and is handy for marinating chicken before cooking it on the barbecue. Add a splash of sake, if you have some.

TANGY GRILLED SALMON WITH PINEAPPLE

FRESH PINEAPPLE REALLY BRINGS OUT THE FLAVOUR OF SALMON. HERE, IT IS COMBINED WITH LIME JUICE TO MAKE A LIGHT AND REFRESHING DISH, WHICH TASTES GREAT WITH WILD RICE.

SERVES 4

INGREDIENTS

grated rind and juice of 2 limes
15ml/1 tbsp olive oil, plus extra
  for greasing
1cm/½in piece fresh root ginger,
  peeled and grated
1 garlic clove, crushed
30ml/2 tbsp clear honey
15ml/1 tbsp soy sauce
4 salmon fillets, each about
  200g/7oz
1 small pineapple
30ml/2 tbsp sesame seeds
ground black pepper
fresh chives, to garnish
wild rice and a green salad,
  to serve

1 Make the marinade. Put the lime rind in a jug (pitcher) and stir in the lime juice, olive oil, ginger, garlic, honey and soy sauce. Taste and add a little ground black pepper. Because of the soy sauce salt will probably not be needed.

2 Place the salmon fillets in a single layer in a shallow, non-metallic dish. Pour the marinade over the salmon fillets. Cover and chill for at least 1 hour, making sure to turn the salmon halfway through.

3 Carefully cut the skin off the pineapple, removing as many of the small black "eyes" as possible. Cut the pineapple into four thick slices. Use an apple corer to remove the tough central core from each slice and cut away any remaining eyes with a small knife.

4 Preheat the grill (broiler) to high. Sprinkle the sesame seeds over a piece of foil and place under the grill for a minute or two until they turn golden brown. Set aside.

5 Grease the grill pan and cover with a layer of foil. Using a slotted spoon, remove the salmon fillets from the marinade and place them in a single layer on the foil. Add the pineapple rings, placing one on top of each piece of salmon.

6 Grill (broil) the fish and pineapple for 10 minutes, brushing occasionally with the marinade and turning everything over once, until the fish is cooked through and the pineapple rings are golden brown.

7 Transfer the fish to serving plates, placing each fillet on a bed of wild rice. Top with the pineapple slices. Sprinkle the sesame seeds over and garnish with the chives. Serve with a green salad.

COOK'S TIPS
• To cook wild rice, put it in a pan of cold salted water. Bring to the boil, then simmer for 30–40 minutes until tender.
• Serve the grilled salmon with a mixed leaf salad. For the dressing, mix 45ml/3 tbsp grapefruit juice with 10ml/2 tsp balsamic vinegar and a pinch each of salt, ground black pepper and sugar, then whisk in 120ml/4fl oz/½ cup mild olive oil.

MONGOLIAN FIREPOT

A FIREPOT PROVIDES A WONDERFUL WAY TO ENTERTAIN. AS WITH FONDUE RECIPES, THE FOOD IS COOKED AT THE TABLE, BUT IN THE HEALTHIER MEDIUM OF STOCK RATHER THAN OIL.

SERVES 4–6

INGREDIENTS
    2 salmon or tuna fillets, each about
        150g/5oz, skinned
    8–12 whole raw tiger or king prawns
        (jumbo shrimp), peeled and
        deveined, with tails on
    6 sachets instant miso soup mixed
        with 1.75 litres/3 pints/7½ cups
        water or the same quantity of fish,
        chicken or vegetable stock
    handful of coriander
        (cilantro) leaves
    2–3 spring onions
        (scallions), sliced
    small bunch watercress, rocket
        (arugula) or young mizuna greens
    50g/2oz/¾ cup enoki mushrooms
    200g/7oz fine egg noodles
    8–12 lemon grass stalks or
        wooden skewers
    soy sauce and wasabi paste or
        horseradish sauce, to serve

For the marinade
    grated rind and juice of 2 limes
    30ml/2 tbsp soy sauce
    2.5cm/1in piece fresh root ginger,
        peeled and finely chopped
    2 garlic cloves, finely chopped
    15ml/1 tbsp clear honey
    1 fresh red chilli, seeded
        and chopped

1 Cut the salmon or tuna fillets into evenly sized 2.5cm/1in cubes and place in a deep serving bowl. Wash the prawns under cold running water, pat them dry using kitchen paper, then add them to the fish cubes.

2 Mix all the marinade ingredients together and add to the bowl of seafood. Toss gently to coat, then cover and leave the seafood to marinate in the refrigerator for at least 2 hours.

3 Pour the stock into a pan, add the coriander and spring onions and bring to the boil. Transfer to a fondue pot and place on a burner at the table.

4 Arrange the salad leaves and mushrooms on serving plates, and put the soy sauce and wasabi or horseradish into small bowls. Add the noodles to the stock at the table and leave to cook.

5 Invite each diner to spear a cube of fish or a prawn on a lemon grass stalk with a salad leaf and a mushroom. This is then submerged in the stock for 1 minute, or until the fish or prawn is cooked, then dipped into the soy sauce and wasabi or horseradish.

6 When the fish and vegetables have all been eaten, serve the remaining stock and noodles in soup bowls.

COOK'S TIP
To make them easier to eat, snip the noodles into short lengths using scissors.

COCONUT SALMON

SALMON IS QUITE A ROBUST FISH, AND RESPONDS WELL TO BEING COOKED WITH STRONG FLAVOURS, AS IN THIS FRAGRANT BLEND OF SPICES, GARLIC AND CHILLI. COCONUT MILK ADDS A MELLOW TOUCH.

SERVES 4

INGREDIENTS

4 salmon steaks, each about
    175g/6oz
10ml/2 tsp ground cumin
10ml/2 tsp chilli powder
2.5ml/½ tsp ground turmeric
30ml/2 tbsp white
    wine vinegar
1.5ml/¼ tsp salt
45ml/3 tbsp oil
1 onion, chopped
2 fresh green chillies,
    seeded and chopped
2 garlic cloves, crushed
2.5cm/1in piece fresh root
    ginger, grated
5ml/1 tsp ground coriander
175ml/6fl oz/¾ cup
    coconut milk
fresh coriander (cilantro) sprigs,
    to garnish
rice with spring onions (scallions),
    to serve

1 Arrange the salmon steaks in a single layer in a shallow glass dish. Put 5ml/ 1 tsp of the ground cumin in a bowl and add the chilli powder, turmeric, vinegar and salt. Rub the paste over the salmon steaks and leave to marinate for about 15 minutes.

2 Heat the oil in a large deep frying pan and fry the onion, chillies, garlic and ginger over a medium heat for 5–6 minutes. Put the mixture into a food processor or blender and process until it forms a smooth paste. If the mixture is too firm add a small amount of oil.

3 Return the onion paste to the pan. Add the remaining cumin, the coriander and coconut milk. Bring to the boil, reduce the heat and simmer the sauce for 5 minutes, stirring occasionally.

4 Add the salmon steaks. Cover and cook for 15 minutes, until the fish is tender. Transfer to a serving dish and garnish with the sprigs of fresh coriander. Serve with the rice and spring onions.

INDEX